Alder Music

Gary L. Saunders

BREAKWATER

Illustrations by the author.

*The Publisher acknowledges the support of the Canada
Council which has helped make this publication possible.*

Canadian Cataloguing in Publication Data
Saunders, Gary L.
    Alder music
    ISBN 0-920911-48-X
I. Title.
PS8587.A86A8 1988   C813′.54   C88-098609-3
PR9199.3.S28A8 1988

In Memory
of
Alden Nowlan

Contents

Foreword

Anyone who delights in the land and the sea, as experienced on the east coast of Canada, should also delight in this book by Gary Saunders. I have been a fan of his ever since I first became aware of his work. Since then I've met him and found out that he was a good fellow to talk with as well as a good fellow to read. Now when I read him I hear his voice. It's a good voice, full of love and laughter, and of pride in the place and people he comes from. You'll find that love, that laughter, and that pride in this book.

Alden Nowlan
Fredericton, N.B.
August 1980

Acknowledgements

For a nice while now I've loved writing. But one does need help along the way. It was good to have a grandmother like Mary Maria Saunders who liked to compose and sing ballads. It helped to have a teacher like Dan Bragg in Grade VII who read us *Prester John* on wintry Friday afternoons, or like Maitland Strangemore in Grade XI who loved the language and was tough about grammar and syntax. In university I was fortunate to have professors like Alec Lucas to open the casements on English literature and encourage me to write. During my early working life I was lucky to travel the woods and streams with a mentor like Danish forester Hans Mandøe, who opened my eyes and ears to many things in natural history and art and music, while I taught him to paddle a canoe and decode Newfoundland English. When I ventured into print it was good to encounter a few understanding editors. Both for publishing my essays and articles over the years and for allowing this reprinting, I owe a special debt to L.S.Loomer, Jim Morrison and Hal Wood of *The Atlantic Advocate*, to Dirk Van Loon of *Rural Delivery*, to Sheila Kaighin and Teddi Brown of *Outdoor Canada* and to Clell Bryant and Lorna Rewjakin of *The Reader's Digest*. I am grateful to Alden Nowlan's widow Claudine for graciously permitting me to use the words he wrote about my first draft. Finally, happy the writer whose family will tell the truth. To their editorial honesty and good sense I owe much of what is best in this collection.

Introduction

I wrote these pieces not so much to keep the wolf from the door as to keep my mind off global catastrophe. While we in eastern Canada are no strangers to calamity, in the 1970s a new brand of unease was creeping in—Strontium 90 in mother's milk, the ticking of Paul Ehrlich's population bomb, the menace of pesticides. Nothing in our experience had prepared us for this. In the old days when disaster threatened we entrusted our lives or property to the hands of Skipper George or Father MacPhee or the midwife. If your boat sprang a leak you could stuff your sweater in the crack and bail like mad—but what could you stuff in the Ozone Hole?

Maybe I was reading too much Carlson and Commoner. For a time I really believed Chaos was Coming. It was in my early forties, and that didn't help. I decided that all I could do was to go easier on the Earth and warn others that the sky was falling. For the first part I settled in the country and went organic—big garden, forty-acre woodlot, chickens, wood stove, coldroom, juice press, compost heap, sun pit. For the second part I took up magazine writing. Setting myself the target of one piece a month about Atlantic Canada, I wrote on childhood, natural history and the environment. In the predawn and midnight stillness, while my wife and children slept and Chaos breathed down my neck, I kept my fears at bay with pen and paper, typewriter and teapot. It did me a power of good. And I was being published. Checks came in from magazines. The discipline of regular writing forced me to examine my experiences, test my knowledge, figure things out. Sometimes a kind reader would urge me on. I kept up the pace for five years, until another project—a book about my father—took all my spare writing time.

Meanwhile a curious thing happened. Though Chaos was no less a possibility, my panic subsided. Perhaps it was the comfort of surveying my rows of corn and cabbage, perhaps my mid-life hormones were throttling down, perhaps all the lonesome hours of writing were paying off. I began to take a longer view. However badly we were treating the Earth and each other, maybe we would have time for a few hurried farewells after all; we might even save the ship.

That was a few years ago. Certainly the news these days is no better. But now people are more sensitive to their environment and more aware of their heritage, especially in Atlantic Canada. Perhaps this is because we have had this love-hate relationship with the land and the sea longer than most other Canadians. We have learned plenty—too much of it the hard way. We also have much to be proud of. As a downeaster I sort of always knew this—it just took me a while to make sure.

This book is a celebration of my journeyings, both spiritual and physical, on the way to finding out. It was first assembled in 1980—when the late Alden Nowlan blessed it—only to be set aside. I offer it here essentially unchanged, except for some new pieces of which I know Alden would approve.

Gary L. Saunders
Old Barns, Nova Scotia
March 1989

Tree Talk

The trees I know, the night I know, the rain I know.

Thomas Merton
Raids on the Unspeakable

• Alder Music •

I must say I like alders. Except for the times I've been in a hurry and they barred the way, alders have given me nothing but pleasure. And not only in the campfire. Everything about this remarkable tree-shrub is congenial to me; its appearance, its attributes, and the company it keeps.

I'll admit at first glance it looks unkempt. Devotees of its more elegant cousin the white birch could be excused for thinking so. The crooked stems curve and sprawl, seldom achieving an upright trunk, let alone tree stature. The mature bark is a nondescript gray-brown. Its wood is brittle and of no commercial value. To the uninitiated, the alder's only claim to attention are the cute mini-pine cones on the upper twigs. Sometimes these find their way into floral arrangements.

Yet we have maligned this humble and harmless dwarf tree beyond measure. Farmers revile it for sneaking into worn-out pastures. Foresters would plow them up and plant larch—though some would grudgingly admit that an alder swamp makes a dandy firebreak. 'Alder swamp'. For many, the very words conjure up visions of swarming mosquitoes and smelly ankle-deep muck.

Isn't it time we made amends? Or at least came to terms? Extermination is out of the question; the alder is far too stubborn and successful. We'll just have to live with it.

As usual we can trust the intuitions of children. While a real forest intimidates them, an alder thicket is just their size. Its springy branches make an ideal jungle. As kids we would watch a Saturday matinee featuring *Tarzan of the Apes*, then troop off to one such thicket to spend the entire summer afternoon dodging ivory hunters and fierce leopards in its risky mazes. In winter, when the swamp would flood and freeze, we played the same games on skates. If I could spare the land I'd plant an alder jungle next to the house just for the children.

Wildlife seems to have the right idea about alders too. On April evenings over most of eastern Canada the winnowing of snipe is as much a sound of Spring as robinsong. As often as not, the snipe's home ground is an alder swamp nearby, where it probes with its long bill for earthworms and other tidbits that live in the rich soil. Woodcock, with their similar habits, are even more partial to alders.

Or come in summertime to look and listen. As your eyes grow accustomed to the bottle-green light under the leafy canopy you may catch a glimpse of the olive-sided flycatcher darting after a mosquito and calling its loud *Quick Three Beers*. Or you may see a yellow warbler flash like a sunray among the branches. And if there's a brook nearby, you may spot a speckled trout lazing in the cool shade while turquoise-and-jade dragonflies rattle their wings in pursuit of gnats.

Autumn is so-so in the alder-woods, if you hanker for colour. There's no fanfare at all. The leaves just curl and fall while still green. Presumably the plant recycles what it needs from them as they lie on the ground in a crunchy brown carpet, smelling deliciously tea-like from their high tannic acid content.

Beavers, intent on laying in winter stores of bark to eat, mostly bypass alders in favour of aspen. But for building dams and lodges they make it their standard construction material. Skillfully weaving and thatching the flexible stems together, the big rodents fashion walls which at the onset of winter freeze rockhard, proof against the strongest meat-eating prowlers.

By November the alder groves seem deserted except for an occasional itinerant jay or crow. The arrival of snow one night only heightens the look of abandonment. Sifting down among the bare branches, it muffles the only notes of colour remaining, until the little glade becomes a study in dark-on-light, more line drawing than three-dimensional reality.

Morning tells a different tale. Everywhere the fresh sheet is eloquent with the typography of animal activity. Over there in boldface capitals I read of the nervous midnight browsing of snowshoe hares. Nearby, in lower-case characters around a dismantled spruce cone, is the same statement by a red squirrel. On this mound a few tiny asterisks tell of a chickadee's quick visit. In

the deeper snow bordering the swamp are the exclamation marks of deer tracks. This dotted line needs no signature to declare that a fox was here. Finally, in fine print at my feet, some notes from the underground; weasel ellipses overprinted on the delicate quotation marks of a field mouse making for the sanctuary of its undersnow tunnels. Picturing that labyrinth of weather-free thoroughfares, I can believe that it got away.

As I said, I'm fond of alders. And the more I learn of its attributes —nitrogen fixer, scented firewood, healer of wounds and diarrhea and sore eyes, natural bonsai forest—the more I cherish it.

As a kid I liked it for more mundane reasons. An alder fishing pole was good for a whole season. The powdered leaves, rolled in brown paper, made quite a good smoke if you could get it lit. With a supple young shoot you could flick iris pods or potato balls at blinding speed toward distant enemies.

Of those childhood uses only one has survived: making whistles. Surely this is one of the least sinful things a grown man can do in the spring. Especially when he does it for children. There's poetry in it.

Last May while leading a Grade Five nature walk I stopped to discuss an alder thicket—and made the tactical error of showing the class how to make a whistle from the sappy green stems. I didn't want the art to die out in suburbia, you see. But for the rest of that hike I did little but make whistles and try to supervise their flashing pen knives.

It's hard to guarantee uniform pitch in alder whistles. You get a variety of notes. Straggling back toward school, we sounded like an orchestra of spring peepers tuning up. My Great Truths of Ecology didn't stand a chance. The kids were making alder music. Pan would have smiled.

— 1976

• Poppletalk •

"And what kind of tree is that, Grandpa?" asks the little Newfoundland tyke out for a summer stroll in the woods with his grandfather. "The one with the quivery leaves."

"Aps, me son," replies the old fisherman with a scowl, "the most useless tree in the woods. No good to build a boat, and worthless in the stove too."

"Oh. But you said the beavers like it. The bark, I mean...?" The boy runs his hand down its green trunk, enjoying the waxy smoothness.

"Aye, that they do. And the beavers is welcome to it!"

Say *popple* for *aps* and this conversation might be overheard anywhere else in eastern Canada. We seem to be down on this one tree. Farmers want it out of their pastures and even woodlots. Lumbermen bypass it. Cottage owners chop it down and plant pines. Foresters, unless they work for a company making veneer or matches or excelsior, call it a weed. Even landscape architects prefer something more exotic. About the only people who are chummy with popple are tree breeders, who refer to it affectionately as trembling aspen, or, if talking shop, as *Populus tremuloides*.

But to most of us a popple or aps by any other name is just as unwelcome. Why this discrimination? A stranger might imagine that it bore deadly fruit or lethal thorns or harboured pests and disease. Nothing of the sort. If aspen has a single trait that annoys us, it is success. Success in treedom means two things: survival and reproduction. By this measure no other native tree can match it. Aspen has the greatest geographical range of any North American species—from Alaska to Newfoundland and south to Mexico.

Moreover, it has close relatives in the Old World, notably *P. tremula*, which the Roman peasant called *popul* (hence *popple* and *Populus*), and which the English of Alfred the Great's day called *aespe* (hence *aps* and *aspen*).

Whatever the source of our low opinion, we may have to revise it. It becomes increasingly clear that trembling aspen is not only one of the most valuable entities of the forest ecosystem, but one of our most promising sources of cellulose for the wood-hungry decades ahead.

You'd never know, to look at it. Apart from its silky gray catkins, which in spring mark it as a member of the willow family, its only notable feature is a crown of 'quivery' leaves. Ultra-sensitive wind-speed indicators, no zephyr is too slight for them to pick up. On the calmest day they flutter constantly, as if the tree were laden with restless green butterflies. On a still night the sound is so like rain that I have often been surprised on waking to find the grass still dry. An old Indian name for aspen meant 'noisy-leaf'. 'Quaking aspen' refers to the same phenomenon.

The explanation for this lies in the way the leaf is attached. Examine a summer twig and you will find that, instead of the sturdy round leaf stem found on most broadleaved trees, aspens have a slender stem compressed like the tail of an eel or the tooth of a comb, and easily bent from side to side. In fact, it is too weak to hold the leaf straight out. Hence the quaking.

A small thing, perhaps; yet it bestows on the humble popple a special quality of ambient coolness and freshness not found in many other deciduous trees. This is nowhere more striking than when one breaks out of the airless gloom of an evergreen thicket on a hot day and steps into an aspen grove with its perpetual imaginary breeze and its perpetual imaginary rain. It's like a draught of cool springwater.

Another pleasant experience is to come upon a beaver pond ringed with aspen. The combination is no coincidence. Beaver relish aspen bark above all others. Plentiful aspen plus unfailing water is their equation for survival. Only when they have gnawed down every usable aspen within a few hundred feet of their lodge will they abandon the dam and pond, leaving it to become at last the fertile flat we call a beaver meadow. In time the water-loving aspen may reforest the meadow. And when the trees are again big enough, other beavers may return to repeat the cycle. Many of the best croplands that greeted our forebears were built up in this way.

Even without beavers, aspens are good for the soil—a fact often overlooked by foresters intent on growing softwood pulp as fast as possible. Directly after one softwood crop is down and hauled to the mill they plant another of the same type. This short-circuits our usual forest succession of coniferous-deciduous-coniferous, a succession which tends to de-acidify and rejuvenate the soil. It also short-circuits the cycle of animal life which normally follows these vegetation changes. The consequence is a loss of diversity and resilience in the ecosystem. In other words, less health.

Nature's scheme for soil rejuvenation is nowhere more evident than after a forest fire. Between Shediac and Buctouche along New Brunswick's Northumberland shore one can drive for miles through nearly unbroken young aspen forest—an exhilarating experience in the fall, when the foliage shimmers like gold sequins in the sun.

This forest sprang up in the 1940s after fire razed stands of mostly softwoods. Although ferns and grasses were quick to appear on the blackened steaming landscape, it was aspen that dominated the rehabilitation process and got everything green again.

Some arrived by air, parachuting in as tiny cotton-tufted seeds wafted from surviving trees up to several miles away. Other seeds travelled by water during June freshets. Most of the trees came from underground, shooting up from special buds on the still living roots, buds that had lain dormant until triggered by greater light and warmer soil after fire let the sunlight in. Because aspens produce extensive root networks, even a sprinkling of this species in a coniferous stand is ample to ensure thickets of suckers after cutting or fire.

So in a few years this area was swept, as it were, by another fire—this time a green and life-giving flame that soon hid the ashes and enveloped the charred trunks and erased all sign of the previous conflagration. Today the burnt trees are part of the soft soil, soil enriched by nutrients lost to the shallow-rooted softwoods but recovered by the aspen's deep roots and non-acid leaf fall. And already one can spot little spruce and fir seedlings underfoot, inching upward in the gentle shade, biding their time until they can overtop their short-lived nurse trees and have the sky all to themselves. Another thirty or forty years and this will be conifer country again. And if we could exclude fire and cutting long enough, it might even become pine-hemlock-yellow birch country, as it was before Europeans arrived.

As we move into a period of ever greater dependence on wood, we would do well to copy such natural cycles in our forest management. After all, farmers long ago learned the wisdom of crop rotation to maintain soil fertility. (Some have forgotten, it is true; but the skyrocketing cost of fertilizers is reminding them.) As society's appetite for wood increases and the budworm competes with us for fir and spruce, we will be forced to rely on hardwoods more anyway. This does not mean we will have to pulp our prime furniture woods like maple and oak. It does mean that we will have to take a second look at this resource, which makes up nearly a third of our total growing stock, and which is under-used while softwood stocks are being over-harvested. Our traditional dependence on softwoods (plus a few select hardwood species) is outmoded. It must give way to a more balanced and ecological approach.

In this process, the humble popple can teach us much. One who sensed this earlier than most was British naturalist Frank Fraser Darling. Touring North American for UNESCO in the 1950s to study our land use practices, he was everywhere impressed with its power to reclaim worn-out soils, to foster other trees, and to promote wildlife. He called it "the great ameliorator," and declared it "a tree to be treated with reverence."

Dropping old prejudices takes time. Yet wildlife biologists recommend favouring aspen. They know that it supports not only beaver, but other bark feeders like mice, snowshoe hare and porcupine, browsers like deer and moose, and bud eaters like ruffed grouse.

So this Cinderella of the forest is coming into its own.

But the traits that most endear aspen to tree breeders and pulpmen are its ease of propagation and its fast growth. Compared to spruce and fir it is fairly easy to grow, springing potato-like from pieces of root set in the ground. It will also grow from treated year-old sprouts, and can be grafted onto quick-rooting stem cuttings of willow or balsam poplar or bigtooth aspen. Moreover, it crosses readily with exotic relatives from Europe and Asia to produce more desirable hybrids. A very sexy tree.

—1977

• Death of a Tree •

It's funny how people get attached to certain trees and hate to see them go.

Hard by the south wall of our house, its wide crown overarching the roof like a parasol, is a big elm we have come to love. With the house, it has weathered the gales of some ninety winters and the suns of ninety summers. In that time it has sheltered more than one family; ours is just the latest to nest under it.

But we thank whoever thought to fetch the sapling and dig the hole and plant this tree so many springs ago. For now on sultry Dog Days its rustling green canopy cools our roof, and in the depths of winter its warm beige bark relieves the wastes of white.

To be sure, it has it faults. Its autumn finery is somewhat on the plain side. Some summers aphids take over the foliage and rain down sticky honeydew to draw flies and begrime our white clapboards; but we can live with that. Some years its thirsty roots invade the septic tank, backing up the contents and forcing me to dig and curse till all hours. But once the hole is refilled and the grass resown I forgive and forget. It also stands too close to the house for comfort; but life is full of perils anyway.

All in all, it would sadden us to lose this elm before its time—which the book says should be a good five decades yet.

Unfortunately we could lose it any year now. Only ten miles away robust elms like ours began to die last summer. For Dutch elm disease has finally reached Nova Scotia, and it is spreading fast. As late as 1968 it was still possible to believe that the province might escape the destruction that overtook the elms of Quebec and Ontario and New Brunswick in the 1950s and 1960s. Then, in 1969, two

diseased elms were spotted in Liverpool on the South Shore. Though both were promptly felled and destroyed and no more cases were reported that summer, between 1970 and 1974 the fatal symptoms showed up in the Annapolis Valley and then in six other mainland counties on more than a hundred trees.

Sooner or later it had to come, of course. Dutch elm disease has ravaged elms all over eastern North America since the 1930s, killing and deforming not only the familiar white elm—the only native Maritime elm—but five other New World species, plus all exotics except two Asian elms. This disease is potent. In New Brunswick it is still spreading and killing trees. New Brunswickers know the pain of losing beloved specimens and pleasant groves. Now it's the turn of Nova Scotians. So far Prince Edward Island has escaped, and Newfoundland has too few elms to need to care.

Like most plagues, Dutch elm disease has travelled far. But Holland was not its place of origin, despite the name. In common with the deadly blight that wiped out America's famous chestnut trees fifty years ago, it came out of Asia. The traffic of the First World War may have helped. In 1919 it appeared in Holland and in northern France. The Dutch pioneered research on its behaviour—and won the doubtful honour of having the disease named after them. By 1927 elms in the south of Britain were infected. Then it hopped the Atlantic, turning up in Ohio in 1930 and in New Jersey two years later.

Since then many more researchers have burned the lab lights late. Though they still have not found a practical cure, they have learned a great deal about how Dutch elm disease operates. For example they know how it kills. It works something like a stroke in humans. The circulation of vital fluids is dammed at some point and beyond that point the parts wither or die. Here the likeness ends, however, because in an elm the stoppage is caused by a yeast-like fungus that stimulates the tree's water-conducting vessels to seal themselves off. (British researchers suspect a poison at work, too.) When the vessels plug up in this way, the leaves on one or more branches suddenly wilt, take on fall colours in midsummer, then die and drop. As the fungus spreads throughout the water-carrying system, branch after branch sickens and dies, until the whole tree succumbs. Young trees may be killed in a month, large old trees may take longer. A few fight if off and survive.

While detection sounds simple, it isn't. Scientists also know that two other elm diseases display the same outward symptoms. This means that before they can confirm or rule out the presence of the causal fungus *Ceratocystis ulmi*, they must culture suspected sapwood material in the laboratory, a process that now takes about a week, and used to take longer. Moreover, *C. ulmi* can go undetected for years in aging trees. Elms die of old age like other organisms; after a while nobody pays much heed to their slow decline. Often it is the sudden yellowing of healthy neighbouring elms that announces trouble. By then the spores can have spread far and wide.

How it spreads is one of nature's ironies. A beetle smaller than a grain of rice is the chief carrier. This beetle feeds on the inner bark of live elms, and breeds between the bark and wood of newly dead elms or newly killed branches. If during feeding or breeding the sticky spores of Dutch elm disease are present, the insect may accidentally pick some up the way a dog picks up cockleburs. Then when it flies to a healthy elm to feed or to a run-down elm to breed, it may infect the tree. If a spore touches live wood, it can be whisked away in the sap stream to multiply and wreak havoc.

So the innocent elm bark beetle, by trafficking in lethal spores, is killing its own food supply.

The disease can also spread underground via root contacts. This happens in Britain where elm hedges are common.

But the long-range transit is supplied by man. Dutch elm disease first entered North America, it is thought, in elm veneer logs from Europe. If so, somewhere in those logs were spore-laden European elm bark beetles. Somewhere in Ohio they left their hiding places and flew through the New World air to a New World elm and found its bark to their liking. Perhaps on the way they met native elm bark-beetles—slighter in build, but otherwise almost identical in form and life habits to their Old World kin. For millennia these native insects had played harmless undertaker to dead and dying American elms. Now, armed with the seeds of destruction, they helped hasten the spread of the fungus.

Ohio being just across Lake Erie from the elm heartland of Ontario, it seemed only a matter of time till the disease reached Canada. Yet it was in the province of Quebec that the symptoms first appeared, fourteen years later in 1944. Ships unloading elm-wood crates near Sorel likely brought the malady from overseas. In fifteen years Quebec had lost more than 600,000 elms in an area bigger than Nova Scotia. By 1946 Ontario elms had been infected from across the Quebec border. And in 1950 the Niagara peninsula and Windsor area were hit by the inevitable incursion from the United States. Closing in thus from two fronts, the disease fairly raced through Ontario's elm-rich counties until in 1963 it embraced an area the size of the Maritimes.

This shows how fast it can move at its worst.

Shall we then lose all our elms? Is our familiar and well-loved white elm, that queen of shade trees, to go the tragic way of the American chestnut, which today survives only as scattered great ghostly trunks ringed with a few miserable green shoots?

Few experts would be so pessimistic as to predict this. The chestnut blight was an extremely virulent, entirely windborne fungus that caught American unawares at a time when knowledge of tree diseases was limited. Dutch elm disease, though very potent

—especially against white elm—is almost wholly insect-borne, it spreads more slowly, and its mechanics are much better understood.

Today the problem is more of mobilizing our knowledge and resources to fight back. This governments at each level are trying to do. At the federal level, the Canadian Forestry Service does excellent work in monitoring the disease, disseminating information, and researching methods of prevention and cure. They have succeeded in developing an injection that can protect individual elms for a short time; but the method is laborious and costly. More promising is their work on controlling overwintering beetles by spraying the lower tree trunks in late summer. In one Ontario study a one percent solution of chlorpyrifos virtually prevented overwintering of beetles.

Provincial governments help where possible with detection, and in some cases tree removal and planting. When the town of Kentville embarked on a massive tree removal scheme two years ago, the Nova Scotia Department of Lands and Forests assisted. Towns like Fredericton and Truro and Windsor have organized tree commissions for better detection, education and sanitation. In fact, Fredericton has over fifteen years of experience in elm-saving, and has made a standing offer to give the benefit of that experience to any town that wants it.

The key word that keeps cropping up in any discussion of Dutch elm disease is sanitation. Sanitation means just that: keeping the trees clean, so that the beetles have no place to breed or to pick up the deadly spores. This in turn means constant vigilance to spot the first signs of old age or storm damage or sudden wilting, and it means following up with prompt removal and destruction or spraying of suspicious material, year after year.

Such a program requires expertise and dedication—and dollars. Caring for small trees is not so bad. The average homeowner can manage it with simple tools and techniques. But the white elm is by nature a large and fast growing tree. (One specimen near Trigonia in Tennessee is more that 160 feet tall and eight feet across.) Most of our street elms were planted before 1900 and are now mature giants. To prune or fell such a tree amid hydro and telephone wires with traffic and pedestrians swirling below demands the skills of a B.C. lumberjack and tree surgeon combined. These skills don't come cheap. Taking down one large specimen can cost over $500. George Goodall, president of Goodall Tree Expert Company, of Portland, Maine, estimated in 1974 that the town of Windsor should budget $15,000 a year to control the disease on its two thousand elms.

But if a town or city can muster the concern and the money, it can save ninety per cent of its elms or better. Fredericton is proof of this. When I first went there as a forestry student in 1954, I was struck by an elegant sign proclaiming it "The City of Stately Elms." Stately was right. Along Queen and Regent and Westmorland and many other streets stood magnificent colonnades that met overhead and hid the sky. Dutch elm disease had not yet arrived. From Up the Hill the city all but vanished under a sea of foliage, with only a scattered church spire poking through to get one's bearings by.

Then in 1961 the fungus struck two trees. Next year two more caught it. In 1964 there were fourteen new cases. By 1967 a total of sixty-four trees had been infected—out of a population of some 7,500 elms. By any standards this was a remarkably low infection rate. What could have been an epidemic was held to little more than a minor rash, while elms up and down the Saint John River Valley died wholesale. Today Fredericton still has most of its stately elms.

The key to this success was sanitation, which happily had been started on a small scale in 1952, before Dutch elm disease even reached New Brunswick. But sanitation did not begin in earnest until a tragedy struck. One squally Sunday morning in 1964, as people filed out of St. Paul's United Church after service, a branch fell from an ancient elm and killed a girl. Her death brought home the realization that trees don't last forever. So Fredericton's older elms were removed, and by the time the disease arrived, its remaining trees were fairly healthy. After that it was mostly just a matter of spotting infections and treating them promptly.

In sharp contrast is the experience of Woodstock, where the first known occurrence of Dutch elm disease in New Brunswick was reported on a single elm in 1957. Like most elmy Maritime towns, Woodstock had enjoyed her trees and never noticed how old they were getting. Meanwhile the disease was at work only fifty-five miles away in Maine. Then when the fateful signs appeared in her very midst, Woodstock delayed removal of the stricken trees too long, despite the urgings of people who knew better. So when the town did start sanitation, *C. ulmi* had a head start.

In the same period when Fredericton lost only sixty-four trees, Woodstock—with a much smaller initial elm population—lost 872.

The lesson is clear for any Maritime town that prizes its elms. Even if they don't have Fredericton's enviable assets—a wealthy citizenry plus two great forestry schools plus a regional office of the

Canadian Forestry Service—they can still do much. Especially in Nova Scotia and Prince Edward Island, where time is on their side.

But what about the elms of the countryside? Unfortunately, they are apt to fare much worse. Because they are scattered over wide areas and much harder to watch than urban trees, the onset of trouble is much easier to overlook. To monitor and treat roadside and farmyard elms alone would be a formidable task. As for wild forest elms, it would be well-nigh impossible. This in turn makes successful urban sanitation harder. Elm bark beetles can't live where all elms are dead. They will strike out for the nearest green or dying trees. Fredericton, now an elm oasis surrounded by dead trees, finds itself beset by increasing swarms of beetles, "Lookin'" (like the boll weevil) "for a home."

For the rural elms the best we can hope for is that in time they will develop a resistant strain. Something like this happened in Britain. Although there was a national felling and sanitation campaign during the 1940s and 1950s, the outbreak seemed to subside partly of its own accord, as if it were running into a more stubborn breed of tree. Maybe after two or three decades the same thing could happen here—or be engineered genetically.

However, there is a catch. Sometime in the 1960s a new and extremely aggressive strain of *C. ulmi* entered Britain and sparked a new epidemic that is now killing even tough rural elms that survived the 1930s outbreak. Ironically, that strain almost certainly came from North America. So the breeder of stronger elms might only be buying time. Genetics wields a two-edged sword.

It is autumn again. Again, in what may be its final normal leaf-fall, our ninety-year-old elm is preparing for winter. Down past the window, tawny and tattered, looping and tumbling, its leaves hurry earthward. Watching them fall, and pondering the strange love affair we have with trees—our genuine individual affection for them versus our collective destructiveness, our capacity to heal versus our capacity to kill—I am moved to ask, with the writer of that truly sad and sadly true lament:

"When will we ever learn?"

—1976

• Lady Birch •

If a popularity poll of Canadian deciduous trees were to be taken, it is a safe bet that one of the top contenders would be white birch. Not only is it one of the best known of all Canadian trees—it is one of the most beautiful and useful. Beautiful not just in one or two seasons—like the maples, which put on a big show of colour each autumn but are drab and gray all winter—but the whole year through. Useful not only in our time, but for millennia before Europeans ever showed up on this continent, and in a variety of ways not matched by any of the other native deciduous species.

White birch has one of the largest distributions of any North American tree—from Newfoundland to Alaska and south into Pennsylvania and even beyond. That's why it has so many names— like paper birch, silver birch, river birch, canoe birch and many more locally. It's something we all share, this tree. And something we have in common with our neighbours to the south, especially in Vermont and New Hampshire. Looking at a typical Christmas card depicting snow and birches with a sleeping village nestled among evergreen hills, it's hard to decide whether we're viewing a scene from rural Cape Breton or the Saint John River Valley or somewhere in New England.

In fact, the white birch is just as beloved by the people of Siberia and Scandinavia, for its close relatives circle the Pole. Lapps use the bark in cloaks and leggings, Norwegians waterproofed their sod roofs with it, Russians tanned leather with it. It's a truly northern tree. And that's why the North American tourist is surprised to come across a grove of it as far south as the Carolinas—at high elevations.

To a tree, being high on a Southern mountain is as good as being high in latitude.

Unlike the elm and maple, this tree doesn't grow to be huge; but it reaches respectable dimensions just the same. On rich, riverside sites it may be more than two feet in diameter and seventy or eighty feet tall. But on a windy hill or seashore it may grow for sixty or seventy years and never get more than twenty or thirty feet tall and a few inches in diameter.

It was the big specimens, now hard to find, which the native people of the region sought when they wanted to build a canoe. They needed large, unblemished sheets to cover the framework amidships —a piece up to six feet long was none too big to reach from gunwale to gunwale. Six feet long translates into a tree more than two feet in the butt. Large sheets also meant less sewing and caulking, a laborious process when working with natural resin and sewing with spruce roots. Another native use of birch bark was for storage containers and drinking cups. The Micmac people folded and sewed it with great skill, often decorating their origami-like creations with exquisite patterns of coloured beads made from dyed porcupine quills.

The native people also used white birch for making toboggans and, in a pinch, snowshoe frames. By cutting thin slats and steaming them, they could bend the wood to whatever shape they required. And today we use it for flooring, spoolwood, clothespins, furniture and firewood.

As a wildlife food source the birch has no great volume of seeds or fruit like some trees, yet it has a number of wildlife followers. Grouse perch in the branches on sunny winter afternoons, nibbling on the buds which contain next year's leaves and flowers in tiny telescoped morsels. Small seed-eaters like various species of sparrows and the junco seek out the tiny winged seeds, either from the papery catkins as they hang from the tree in autumn or from the ground or snow crust in winter.

When we think of tree syrup we automatically think sugar maple. Among winemakers, at least, birch has its devotees, especially in Britain. Our largest birch, the curly or yellow birch, produces a sap with a wintergreen taste which is not very palatable. But the white birch has a plain, sweet flavour that transmutes in the winemaker's skilled hands to a pleasant dry white wine.

But it is as the most elegant hardwood of the boreal forest that Canadians prize the white birch. Europeans and Britons do too—

Coleridge called it "The Lady of the Woods" and the English encyclopedist Hugh Johnson raved over its fall foliage, calling it "the purest, most sovereign gold of any tree's." Without those sovereign accents in Canada's landscapes many of the best-loved autumn scenes of the famous Group of Seven would have looked dull.

My own favourite setting for this tree is on a snowy winter hillside against dark evergreens—preferably at night, and preferably with a moon. Then you get a subdued but dazzling interplay of muted white-on-white all interlaced with dark shadows and darker twigs. If there's a bit of snow falling in big, lazy flakes, so much the better. Even the most embittered winter-hater has to agree that it's almost enough to make it all worthwhile.

—1986

• To Whittle an Alder Whistle •

I f someone asked me right now who first showed me how to make an alder whistle, I couldn't say. My father? Probably not, because when I was ripe for such lore he was away a lot working. My mother? No; women didn't seem to whittle much when I was a kid. My brother? He was probably too busy chasing girls. An uncle—I mean the authentic, blood-related sort? That's a possibility. And it could have been any one of several peripheral uncles of the sort so common in those tribal days before the nuclear family and the old folks' home undermined their status, one of those Uncle Bobs or Uncle Rays of indeterminate linkage who seemed equally beloved by our parents and us.

But no; when I come right down to it, my guess is that it was one of my grandfathers. They were different as day and night. The gruff, shopkeeper one? Couldn't have been him, for with all his hurrying and worrying he hardly knew our names. (Or so we thought then. Later we found out different, found out the reasons for his worries, learned how many people he was carrying on credit with no hope of repayment.)

So that leaves the other one, the impossibly tall, stooped giant with the weathered face, twinkling brown eyes and beaked nose, the one who all his life had made fish barrels in which to ship salt cod to Spain. This gentleman did stay with us one winter. I remember him sleeping on the daybed in the kitchen, his wool-stockinged Size Twelve feet dangling over the end because it was too short for his lanky frame. And that spring, when the meadow flooded, he did whittle me a sailboat. Yes, it might well have been him.

Whoever it was, I wonder if he realized the significance of his act to me, the small human person seated at his knee on the doorstep, completely absorbed in the purposeful movements of strong, calloused hands and shining knife blade. I cherish the notion that such innocent rituals help keep human society from flying apart. Out of the strong came forth sweetness. Out of the common wood came a magical note, a bond with the past. So now I too carve whistles for small people.

The trick is to get the bark off and on again without cracking it. Spring, when the buds and catkins are swelling and the bark is slippery with rising sap, is the only time to do this. If you don't know alders by their bark or buds or new leaves, ask someone, or consult a book. Brook valleys and wet fields are the place to look. Choose a nice smooth sprout that is free of twigs or bumps for at least three inches, and as thick as a cigar. With a sharp blade, slice downward at an angle while holding the branch from above. Trim off any excess twigs until you're left with a manageable stick six or eight inches long. That will give you enough for a whistle at each end—in case the first fails, which is likely.

Before removing the bark you must shape the mouthpiece. A forty-five-degree cut with no rough edges is about right. (It may be that you cut it that way in the field.) Square off the sharp end a bit so the bark won't fray. Now score the bark all the way around the stem about two inches back from the tip. The best way to do this is to hold the blade against the bark with one hand, and roll the stem against the blade with the other. This gives a good straight line. Repeat a quarter inch farther along. Slit between the marks and peel off the resulting ring of bark. This gap will let you adjust for better sound later on.

Lay the piece on your knee and tap it gently but firmly all over with a rounded object like the handle of your knife (sharp corners will ruin the final product), going back as far as the ring of bare wood, and turning the stem as you go. Grasping the tapped portion in one hand and the untapped in the other, twist. The tapped part should come unstuck and turn, like a screw-top bottle cap. If it doesn't, tap and twist some more. When it does (as it will, if you don't crack it first), you can easily pull the bark off in one piece.

Just before you do that, line up the bark as it was and carefully remove a small lens from the top with the blade tip a half inch back from the lip, taking care to cut slightly into the wood. This lens-shaped hole will be the whistle's air outlet. (Had we cut it earlier

G. SAUNDERS/83

we would have risked breaking the bark while tapping or twisting.)
Fresh alder bark is fragile. It also dries and shrinks rapidly, so I make
a habit of holding the sleeve in my mouth like a cigar and breathing
through it to keep it moist while I finish the whistle.

The next step is to carve a chamber in which the air can resonate.
Its length can be varied (the longer the chamber the deeper the pitch),
but the end toward the lip should always lie right under the air
outlet. This is where my hint about cutting the wood slightly comes
in; it leaves a mark to guide you. Slanting the blade about 45 degrees
and parallel to the lip, bear down (on a firm surface, not your knee)

with a rocking motion until it reaches the center of the stem. An inch or so away, make a second cut facing the first but opposite in slant and half as deep. With the blade still in the wood, prise out the chip. Repeat until the chamber has an even depth. Trim off any loose slivers.

Now there is only one step before you slip the bark sleeve back in place. You still need an opening to get the air into the chamber. Make this by shaving off a layer of wood the thickness of a dime between the chamber and the lip.

By this time the wood surface will be almost dry. Before reassembling, wet it in your mouth (alders contain nothing poisonous, only tannin—like tea) so it won't stick to the bark. Slide the bark back on and adjust until the air-hole is above the near end of the chamber. Puckering your lips (taking care not to cover the air vent), gently blow into the whistle. A clear sweet note should sound. If it doesn't, fiddle with the bark sleeve until you hear something other than air escaping. If even that doesn't work, remove the sleeve and pare the air intake a trifle deeper. Wet the wood again and repeat the test, again adjusting if necessary. With luck you'll be rewarded. If success still eludes you, put it down to experience and right away make another. There's nothing wrong with the design. But even veteran whistle whittlers fail. Patience; it will come.

When it does, you'll be able to indulge in one of the purest pleasures of springtime, that of making a whistle for a youngster. From experience I can affirm that this coaxing of sound from an ordinary stick is one of the most satisfying of acts for all concerned. It can't be the music alone; there's only a single note. Yet I've known adults—even teachers—to exclaim with delight when finally they heard it. For the more inventive there are other designs and different woods to be tried. Willow is good, and probably some other species are too.

But for a start, try the humble alder. Follow my recipe, and take along a youngster or two. It will make the world a saner place.

—1983

• Window Tree •

Tree at my window, window tree,
My sash is lowered when night comes on;
But let there never be curtain drawn
Between you and me.

Robert Frost

N evertheless, when your window tree starts dropping large branches on the driveway every time a big wind comes along, you know it's time to terminate the relationship. And that's how it is with the maple outside our bedroom window. I've known for some time. Yet I keep putting off the dirty work, the actual felling. Actually, it shouldn't have to be done for decades yet. At ninety years of age a healthy sugar maple is still in its prime. But ever since it was planted it has been shaded by a bigger maple to the south. The years of sibling rivalry have taken their toll.

Fortunately for my resolve, it never was a pretty tree. It looks more like a giant feather duster than a proper sugar maple. The side branches, seeking light at all costs, stretched out at the expense of the top ones. Yet homeliness has its charms, enough at least to let me dawdle for another day.

After all, it's not like cutting down a strange tree in the woods. There are things to consider.

For instance, there's the responsibility of cutting down a tree that someone else planted when one's grandparents were toddlers; not only planted, but apparently brought from some distance—since sugar maples aren't found naturally along this Fundy shore where we live. In those days they couldn't order them from a nursery either.

And what of historical sentiment? This tree is almost as old as our country. Most of the events of our history could be ticked off on its crowded rings. The saw would have cut in only an inch or so before it passed my own birth year, and it would still have nearly a foot of wood to cross on the way to the pith. It gives one pause.

Closer to home, there are the inevitable personal ties that develop from close acquaintance. Most of us think twice before breaking such attachments. We know that once we do there will be for years afterward sights and sounds and smells and textures that trigger memories, some nice, some not. Already, after only nine years' sojourn by this tree, I can recall some of both.

Tapping maple sap is one of the nice memories. With only two trees we never got much. It was more ritual than anything else. And after seven years the number of tap holes in the smaller tree began to worry me. But it was worth it, if only for such things as the sight of our big brown dog standing on his hind legs and carefully lapping sap from a pail. Had he heard us laughing from inside the house I'm sure he would have wagged his tail apologetically and made himself scarce.

Another nice tree-memory concerns the October day one of our boys Discovered a Tree. "Come see this, will you!" chuckled my wife, motioning me to the window. There under the feather-duster tree stood three-year-old Matthew lost in thought. He was leaning back so far on his heels, gazing up into the foliage, that it seemed he would topple backwards. I thought of the Druids and their sacred trees. He stood thus for some minutes, the yellow leaves drifting down around him.

The children would certainly miss their rope swing. I tied it where one of the lower branches takes a graceful dip out over the driveway. Ever since, there's been this patch of bare pounded earth in the grass beneath—a sure sign of popularity. How the branch got bent that way I don't know. Maybe somebody had a swing on it when it was still too small—say during the First World War or earlier.

Except for the falling branches, the unpleasantries of living near a large old tree are mostly minor. You get used to the strange sounds day and night. Sometimes with an east wind there are mysterious rustlings along the eave and strange tappings up and down the gable. On still Sunday mornings woodpeckers hammer out coded messages. In time you come to believe in tree spirits. Then there is the small talk. Trees go in for inordinate amounts of this. In summer, rain is a favourite topic. Light breezes come up for frequent whispered conferences too. In the fall there's a lot of raspy gossip about the way John Frost is handling the current crop of leaves. But it is in winter that the really serious topics are taken up. Then we hear everything from arthritic creaks to sickbed moans and even an occasional ear-splitting report as the frost wreaks its vengeance some bitter night. And often we fall asleep to the deep thrum of strained fibers as a blizzard plays wild rasgueados on taut branches.

Without a window tree all this could cease.

And what of replacement? Clearly I would have to replant. But with what? Since the big tree to the south is likely to shade the ground for decades yet, the newcomer would have to be content with half-light. This suggests a conifer, a red spruce maybe. Or, better still, a hemlock? Then what would a hemlock provide instead of maple syrup? Would it get along with the big maple? How much would it complain in the night? Could it guarantee a branch suitable for a rope swing, and how many years would that take?

Time: there's the rub. Even the fastest growing trees take their own sweet time. This goes against the modern grain. Their indifference to time irks us. We'd much prefer an instant tree. And every single one we plant confronts us with the prospect of our own demise.

Is *that* why I keep putting off this chore?

Well, then. Fetch my power saw. Is there gasoline mixed? Is there chain oil in it? Got a rope in case the thing tries to fall across my neighbour's pasture fence? A felling wedge and axe in case it pinches the bar? Has the swing been moved to the other tree? And you're sure there are no robins' nests in the crown?

All affirmative. No turning back. The saw snarls and spits white chips, then brown. The old trunk shudders as no wind ever shook it, leans, falls, sprawls all over the driveway.

Old tree, we'll not soon forget thee. With gratitude for past pleasures given and for services rendered—not the least being thy final bequest of cordwood to warm us for a month this winter—we'll keep thee in our hearts. And, later, we'll plant another.

—1978

Fellow Tenants

Only the mountain has lived long enough to
listen objectively to the howl of a wolf.

Aldo Leopold
A Sand County Almanac

• Hawk •

It was our boy Danny who brought the young male sparrow hawk home. He'd found it flapping helplessly on the road, trying to fly back to the nest it had left too soon. Danny approached us nervously with his prize, because ever since his mother was chased by a turkey-gobbler as a child, she's had this thing about birds. Feathers give her the shivers. She'd rather pick up a snake.

Danny needn't have worried. She loved the little hawk at first sight. Something in the lustrous dark eyes of this robin-sized bird of prey, something in his calm and kingly mien, made her forget the feathers. Even now her eyes brim at his mention.

For one thing, he was exceedingly handsome. And the bird book said he was a true falcon: *Falco sparverius*, diminutive cousin of the royal peregrine who had flown from lordly wrists to strike down grouse for the lordly board. All of this 'Hawk'—we never did get around to naming him properly—seemed to know as he perched on one foot in his makeshift cage, crowned and winged in blue-gray, a chestnut mantle about his shoulders, his whole attire barred with jet black like ermine tails.

With such a pedigree perhaps he could afford to look civilized. For he eyed us not with that accusing golden stare of eagles and owls, but with a look suggesting whimsical intelligence—a look which, in humans, one might put down to a sense of humour.

For another thing he was fastidious. Your average captive robin is too scared to risk bathing. Not so *Falco*: the first time we offered him enough water he plunged right in, dunking and splashing in apparent glee, evoking giggles from his audience of unfastidious children. He often washed his face, too.

And he ate with gusto. In captive birds this means a lot. We've been through so many bird tragedies. Every spring comes this parade of orphaned sparrows and fledgling robins borne by anxious foster parents. Stuffed all day with worms and beetles and love, fretted over at bedtime, they invariably stop eating and keel over around the third day, ending up under popsicle-stick crosses in our crocus bed.

This bird was different. With the critical third day already past, he was still avid for raw hamburger and chicken. Raw sparrow we never offered, since the book said mice and insects were much more to his fancy. Sure enough, he accepted a mouse. Live green grasshoppers pleased him best of all; his soft appreciative *klee-klee-klee* told us so. With such an appetite we knew he'd make it —unless the cats, who liked to sleep atop his cage, got him first.

We began to relax and enjoy Hawk's antics. Like the time we showed him his first mirror. It was in the bathroom over a glass shelf full of the usual bric-a-brac. Without warning he screamed and attacked. The rival mirror-bird gave blow for blow, slash for slash. Before they were done, the floor was strewn with toothbrushes, lipstick tubes and talcum powder and we were bent with laughter. Later we tried him with a mirror propped on the kitchen table; but this time it was no go. Failing to stare the intruder down, he simply hopped behind and inspected the back of the glass. I like to think he figured it out....

His vision was astounding. If I flashed sunlight off a hand mirror in a darkened room, his eye would track the ray's every lightning move as if tied to it by an invisible wire. We feared he'd swivel his neck off.

We talked to him a lot. I won't say he ever replied, but he would pump his head rapidly up and down, or tilt it right and left like an inquisitive puppy. Perhaps it amused him to see us teeter.

Once we took him on a three-hundred-mile car trip. That was the time a kid offered in vain to buy him. Hawk was no trouble, and seemed to enjoy being with us. But although I joked about training him to hunt, we never intended to keep him.

By the time the apple blossoms had faded he was visibly maturing and could even fly a little. When the cats were safely outside, Danny would sometimes let him flap about the house. Recapturing him was easy, for he liked to ride on hands or shoulders. Once when we lost him for a few hours he was found sleeping, head under wing, on the bar in an upstairs clothes closet.

One day he didn't wish to be hand-fed any more. I decided that the time had come. When I took him outside and perched him in the apple tree, however, he cringed. My wife was just as happy to defer the day of parting, but we all knew it must be soon. We were getting too attached.

A week later, the day came. I was away when it happened. Hawk had become very vocal and agitated. Danny, sensing the moment, took him outside again and offered him meat. He came out of his cage, he took the meat, he looked around, he shivered. Then with a spring he was in the air above his master's head, circling silently as if on a taut cord. Moments later the invisible cord snapped, releasing our falcon to rocket upward in superb flight until he dwindled to a swallow, a fly, a mote—and was gone. Stiff-necked from peering aloft, the children sniffled and my wife wept.

After that, I saw him only once. It was a few days later. He was perched on a post, probably hunting insects. As I talked my way gingerly toward him he kept tipping his head in that comical way we'd come to love. At five paces he cried the characteristic, sharp *killy killy killy* and shot away in a low skimming arc across the green summer fields.

But I had an idea. I'd build a nest box that he and his future mate could occupy next spring. It would be our small gesture to the declining falcon tribe.

The following March I lifted the prescribed structure into place on its twenty-foot pole, and we waited. And waited. They never came.

I suppose my effort wasn't entirely wasted. For several springs now I've played landlord to a bunch of squalling starlings. *Sturnus vulgaris.* Mere birds.

—1975

• Unkemptitude •

One May morning while dashing my face with cold water to wake it up I became aware of the song of a robin. So lovely was it that I opened the bathroom window to listen. The song went on for some minutes, a cascade of bright liquid notes with no fixed score, variations on some theme of joy known only to robins I suppose. It came from a tall spruce next door.

By the time I'd towelled my face dry I was fully awake. With binoculars I saw the singer leave his treetop and disappear into a brushy fencerow bordering the far side of our lane. Here I discovered a nest in progress. Later I noted that robins weren't the only birds interested in this piece of real estate. A fox sparrow, a chipping sparrow and several warblers were frequent visitors too. I even spotted a hummingbird.

"Now what's so special about that scrap of land?" I asked myself. It was too tiny for a woodlot and too steep to mow or plow. As far as I could see it just caught snow in the winter and made the lane harder to shovel out. Still, to the birds it was special.

For the first time in ten years of walking and driving and shovelling past this fencerow, I began to really *see* it. Oh, I'd admired the wild roses in mid summer, but that was about all. So I did a slow tour. Plants are one of my hobbies, yet I wasn't prepared for what I found. In the space of a hundred feet I counted no fewer than eighteen species.

The significance of this hedgerow dawned on me. Apart from providing different kinds of living space, every different plant means a different kind of food; not only its seed or fruit, but the insects it attracts. Just as roses attract aphids and tomatoes draw hornworms, so every weed and wild plant has its own following of bugs. I guess I had known this principle all along. I just hadn't drawn the logical conclusion: the greater the diversity of plants in this and other hedgerows hereabouts, the richer the medley of songs when I opened my bathroom window.

Even without its fragrant pink blossoms, wild rose was easy to identify by its glossy multiple leaflets and its prickly stems. Some of its relatives were present too. I saw choke cherry—the one whose August fruit puckered the roof of my mouth when I was a kid—wild raspberry, wild spiraea or steeplebush, and even a couple of apple tree saplings.

How did they all get there? In each case the seeds are too large to sail on the wind. The apple trees likely owed their presence to an apple core someone tossed away; what about the rest?

Of course—birds did it. Another example of nature's economy of means—"There's no such thing as a free lunch." It is a fact that all one has to do to start a natural hedge across a bare field is to stretch a single strand of wire between posts and wait a few years.

Most of the other plants I found came by bird-power too. They included buttercup, vetch (the little blue-flowered wild pea, thought to be equivalent to the *tare* in Jesus' parable about the wheat and the tares), orchard grass, and that champion of weeds, couch or twitch grass.

The wind brought all the rest. Canada goldenrod and New England aster, those harbingers of the Fall, certainly arrived that way. Both bear silk-tufted seeds that waft about the autumn countryside after their August flowers have faded. Dandelion, best-known of such wind-travellers, was also in evidence. In fact it was the only one in flower yet. After a long cold winter its sunny blossoms didn't look half bad. Among the shrub representatives there was one kind of willow, the silvery-leafed beaked willow. Downy alder was represented too.

Of forest trees there were four sugar maple saplings (offspring of a big maple by our house), two yellow birch, a grey birch, and even a white spruce. The spruce had some budworm in it.

A closer look uncovered timothy, tansy, yarrow, cinquefoil, hawkweed, curled dock and stitchwort. Others, like ox-eye daisy and black-eyed Susan, revealed their presence later.

Thus I discovered, right under my nose on one tiny scrap of 'wasteland', more species of plant life than is found on the whole surrounding hundred acres of manicured cropland. And they were there only because the steep bank was uneconomic to farm. If society ever becomes hungry enough or efficient enough, all steep banks will be farmed. Already, impedimenta like fencerows are being removed to speed the process of plowing, harrowing, seeding, fertilizing and harvest. In parts of Nova Scotia's Annapolis Valley the decline of hedgerows and brushy corners has been drastic. Mechanized farming is above all *clean* farming. This means that pheasants and other hedge-dwellers must seek elsewhere, which leads to overcrowding and starvation.

When we came to live on our half-acre plot amid these fields, I decided to imitate nature and try to start my own wild hedgerow to windward of our new garden. Wind is a factor to contend with here; it funnels up the Bay of Fundy as if bent on sweeping man and his doings away. The bird-on-wire routine was too slow for me. Besides, the robins were eating our strawberry crop before *we* could get to it. To lure them away, I wanted something fast-growing. Pin cherry, it was reported, would do the trick. The birds were supposed to like its tart fruit even better. After I planted a couple of dozen and they bore fruit I found this to be more or less—often less—true. But pin cherry is short-lived and prone to black-knot fungus. So I've been interplanting other things like mountain-ash, serviceberry and elder. I once tried hawthorn, but removed them when I learned that they harbour apple maggot.

It's a slow process, this imitating nature. Especially when you're out of practice and have all but forgotten the rules. But it's the way we have to go.

—*1979*

• Rudolph the Red-Nosed Whitetail •

D on't tell the children but Rudolph the Red-Nosed Reindeer is an imposter. So are Dasher and Dancer and the rest. Far from being reindeer, they are really whitetail deer—and Disney versions at that. The whitetail isn't even native to Atlantic Canada, but was imported like so many other things from farther west and south. Our true reindeer (the woodland caribou) became extinct in the Maritimes and was drastically reduced in Newfoundland over fifty years ago.

I mention this not to be picky, nor to start a campaign to install caribou on our Christmas cards. Anyway Rudolph and his troupe have crept into our hearts, and the kids love them. But I do think we lose something vital to regional identity when we let native wildlife fade from our folklore—or worse, from our landscape. We tend to do both. Many of us wouldn't know a caribou if we saw one. And most of us would be surprised, I suspect, at the number of species that have disappeared from the Atlantic Provinces since our ancestors arrived. I was. Maybe knowing about those losses will help prevent further extinctions.

Caribou isn't an isolated case. We once had our own wolf, too. Because both were linked as predator and prey in one of nature's marriages of necessity, they disappeared together. Our ancestral Old World dread of wolves helped, too. Here and there you can still meet an old Maritimer who remembers this magnificent wild dog. And the last one ever seen alive around my home village in Newfoundland was encountered around 1876 by a housewife when she went to the brook for water. The ruffian had gorged himself on salt herring and was helplessly bloated from trying to quench a raging thirst. Naturally she ran and got an axe and killed him.

We had our own lion, as well. Maybe we still do. Bruce Wright claims to have documented the eastern cougar's presence in New Brunswick, and Nova Scotia's biologists get numerous unconfirmed reports. Yet if this powerful but shy cat still exists here, it must be close to extinction.

In Nova Scotia man's activities have endangered another large cat, the lynx. Since the Cape Breton causeway was built in 1955, ice-bridges forming to the north in Canso Strait have allowed the lynx's more aggressive southern cousin, the bobcat, to invade. Out-competed, the lynx has retreated to the snowy highlands.

Moose and black bear, both of which can benefit from man's activities, have fared better—except on Prince Edward Island. There the settlers soon wiped them out. Today the Garden of the Gulf supports no wildlife bigger than a beaver.

Nova Scotia's beaver had a close brush with extinction. Naturalist Titus Smith Jr., after extensive travels there in 1801-02 looking for naval stores, declared that they were "almost destroyed, although there is perhaps no country where they have been more numerous heretofore." After 1907 strict laws and judicious beaver transplants rescued this valued furbearer. But even today it is scarce in the eastern mainland counties.

Two other furbearers that suffered violent decline in Atlantic Canada are the fisher and marten of the weasel tribe. Both survive only as secretive remnant populations. Fisher introductions from Maine have improved that animal's chances in Nova Scotia; otherwise it might have gone the way of its larger relative the giant sea mink, which was trapped into oblivion and is now found only in museum cases.

Museum cases recall the tragedy of the great auk, the big flightless penguin that once teemed around our coasts. "In less than half an hour we filled two boats full of them," wrote Cartier in 1534. The scene of this first recorded slaughter was Funk Island off northeast Newfoundland, a principal breeding ground. After three hundred years of merciless plunder for meat and feathers

and even eggs, they were gone from the face of the earth.

Handsome pearl-gray plumage and tasty meat led the diminutive Labrador sea duck to the same fate. In the 1700s even New Englanders were outfitting vessels to collect it for hat and table during its flightless breeding season. Today the world's museums hoard forty-three specimens.

These are some of the skeletons in our wildlife closet. We needn't dwell on the man-caused troubles of ospreys and eagles; the future of Newfoundland's Arctic hare, or of the Saint John River's rare shortnosed sturgeon; the fate of Sable Island's wild ponies or western Nova Scotia's unique Atlantic whitefish population. It's enough to say that as a people we have been hard on our wildlife.

True, most of the damage was done by our forefathers who, with guns and traps and clubs, openly and year-round, out of fear and greed and hunger, pursued these hapless creatures to the brink of extinction and beyond. But we shouldn't feel smug. Our carefree, outdoorsy beer ads lie to us. Despite our prattle about environment and ecology, and our tax-deductible donations to save-the-wildlife funds, the crimson pioneer streak still colours our collective attitudes. Thanks to saner game laws and quotas, hunting and trapping are no longer the main threat. The threat today is from land abuse. Habitat destruction is our specialty. Unlimited proliferation of four-lane highways, shopping plazas, dams, and toxic chemicals can destroy wildlife just as effectively as our ancestor's cruder methods. Unfortunately, bulldozers are far harder to halt than muskets. And like our forebears we have to make a living.

I guess it all comes down to a sense of values. How much is a cougar or caribou worth? Not in dollar values—but for itself. Could it be that a true assessment here would reform our other values and sharpen our sense of regional identity? I don't know; but for me those animals express deep heraldic truths about us that no Bambi-eyed whitetail comes near to expressing. I would emblazon them on our coat-of-arms, if not on our Christmas cards.

That's why I say—keep an eye on that Rudolph.

—1975

• God's Dog •

Any night now I expect to hear wolf music in my own back yard. It won't be the same wolf music that made our forefathers reach for their muskets nor the kind that scared the youngsters in their bunks. In fact, it will be a serenade we never expected to hear in these parts except in a western movie. Yet it will send shivers down the spine of the most rational listener. It will be, of all things, the song of a coyote.

For coyotes are moving into these parts. It's nothing new. Since the late 1950s there have been rumors and unconfirmed reports. As early as 1966 a dog-like animal was killed by a car near Debec in Carleton County, New Brunswick, and later identified as a coyote. In 1970 one was shot not far from Moncton. Two years later a trapper caught one near Edmundston.

But while the coyote's presence may not be remarkable, its buildup and spread is worth watching. In 1977 thirty were killed in New Brunswick and, for the first time, two turned up in Nova Scotia.

What's going on? Why this sudden influx of a western predator? Are they come to stay? What will they do to our native wildlife—and our sheep? What can be done about them?

What's going on has not been all that sudden. Strange as it may seem, it started when we felled the first tree to make the first clearings. "Letting sunlight in the swamp," the settlers and lumbermen called it. From that day the age-old balance of the landscape began to shift from virgin forest to open space, first along the eastern seaboard and then westward. For the western coyote, whose natural range covers prairie and brushland from Alaska to Costa Rica, it was an invitation to fresh pastures. Coyotes, like humans, prefer open sunlit spaces to thick forest. Under mature trees the light is dim, the air cool. Except to hide or escape bad weather, few animals come here. There is little to eat. But out under the open sky, in areas of brush, marsh, choppings and farmland there are berries, insects, mice, shrubs, rabbits, snakes, frogs, seeds, deer—a supermarket of wildlife goodies.

One of Nature's laws is that Vacuums Must Be Filled. Anyone who has tried to keep dandelions off a new lawn knows how strictly it is enforced. The coyote is simply obeying that law.

Some say the coyote is replacing our now extinct timber wolf, *Canis lupus*. This seems unlikely. The two have different lifestyles. Wolves prefer to live in mature forest remote from man's doings, preying on big animals like moose, deer and caribou. The eastern coyote likes clearings and second-growth forest and hunts small animals like rabbits and mice and groundhogs for the bulk of its diet.

Anyway, coyotes first appeared in eastern Canada around 1906, crossing into Ontario from the Lake States. In the 1920s coyote or 'prairie wolf' pelts started showing up in Hudson Bay Company stores in northern and central Ontario. Following the shores of Lake Erie and Lake Ontario they loped east into New York's Adirondack Mountains, north across the frozen St. Lawrence into Quebec, and east again into Vermont, New Hampshire and Maine. By the 1930s and 1940s coyote-like animals were being reported throughout upper New England. From Maine and Quebec they entered New Brunswick and Nova Scotia.

Although individual coyotes are great travellers (one tagged specimen turned up four hundred miles away), this five-hundred-mile journey across four states and four provinces was done slowly, litter by litter, over the span of a human lifetime, like ink spreading on a blotter.

There was even time for the animal to evolve new characteristics. The eastern coyote is considered a sub-species of the western or true coyote (*Canis latrans*). It is heavier and darker and has a bigger skull. Some even say it has a deeper bark. Biologists think that on the way east and north it may have bred with a smallish sub-species of timber wolf found near the Great Lakes. As proof they cite the fact that the two have produced fertile offspring in captivity. Crosses with domestic dogs are also common, but their genetic input is thought to be slight, because staggered mating cycles in the offspring mean that pups are born in mid-winter instead of spring. Most of them die of cold. Also working against the build-up of coydogs is the fact that hybrid males, unlike true coyote males, make indifferent fathers and spouses, abandoning the female soon after she gives birth.

Are coyotes here to stay? Wildlife managers think so. David Cartwright, fur biologist with the New Brunswick department of natural resources, considers them "well and permanently established here." Neil van Nostrand, his counterpart in Nova Scotia, agrees. They figure that for an animal so elusive and trap-shy to be taken in such numbers, there must be a good many more around.

So it seems we have a new wildlife neighbour. The least we can do is to get to know it better.

The coyote comes with almost mythic credentials. Brother to the domestic dog and the untamed wolf, he has always fascinated North American man. The Aztecs (who named him *coyotl*) carved his image in their temple walls. His deeds are enshrined in the folklore and legend of many Indian tribes as the personification of cunning and trickery. He has been adapted to television as the hero's wily foe in Warner Brothers' TV series *The Roadrunner Hour*. And lately he has become the butt of bumper sticker graffiti ("Eat Canadian Lamb—10,000 Coyotes Can't Be Wrong") imported from the States.

The survival equipment of this little wolf is formidable. Although neither large nor powerful (the average weight of more than 250 Ontario coyotes was only thirty-two pounds, though some exceeded fifty), it has three aces up its sleeve: speed, cunning and adaptability. You'd never know it to look at one. You'd say it was just a skinny, small German shepherd with rough, grizzled fur and bushy black-tipped tail.

A western coyote was once clocked at forty-three miles an hour. It is one of the few mammals that can run down a jack-rabbit. But it does not rely on speed alone. It is nothing for one coyote to decoy a gopher out of hiding so that another hiding nearby can nab it. One was even seen busily levelling the protective mounds around some gopher holes while a rainstorm threatened, then piling the earth in a V-shaped dam on the uphill side. When the cloudburst broke, the resulting flood forced the normally flood-proof prairie dogs gasping to the surface—and into the waiting coyote's jaws. This wild dog can also catch frogs like a raccoon, fish trout like a grizzly, and spring traps like a wolverine.

Nova Scotia's first known coyote happened to be a sheep killer. In thirteen months from June 1976 to July 1977 near Saltsprings in Pictou County this animal took seventy lambs and sheep from under the nose of Harry Mowatt, a veteran hunter and trapper assigned by the government to get him. The killer, a thirty-four pound male as it turned out, quickly learned to recognize Mowatt's truck and would seldom attempt a kill when the vehicle was parked anywhere nearby. So Mowatt took to sitting all night on a farmer's tractor. Even then he had to use an Armed Forces 'Starlite' rifle scope, because the coyote would not face a light like other night predators. "During 1975," declared Mowatt, "I live-trapped or killed fifteen bears that were breaking into beehives and causing other problems, and it was easier than to kill this one coyote." From such cunning arose the Mexican phrase *muy coyote* to describe great shrewdness—what my grandmother would call "wonderful cute."

Like the wolf, it is thought to mate for life. The male is a devoted spouse and parent, bringing food to the female while she is pregnant and working hard to feed and raise the three to ten pups, which are born in a den in early spring. Babysitting and wet-nursing are often shared by uncles and aunts. If one or both of the parents are killed, relatives and even strangers will pitch in to bring up the orphans.

Hunting is usually in relays, not packs. The game is driven in a circle past fresh runners stationed at suitable points, until the kill is made. Although meat-eaters by nature, coyotes will down almost anything; insects, grass, berries, apples, garbage, even pine needles. Rabbits and mice seem to be staples, and dead deer are eaten whenever found, especially in winter when other meat is scarce. Such catholic tastes mean that coyotes can survive almost anywhere, even in a metropolitan area like Toronto. Los Angeles residents complain that coyotes raid their garbage cans and even kill their cats and dogs.

Without such speed, cunning and adaptability the coyote could not have survived contact with man, especially sheep-raising man. It would surely have gone the way of its larger cousin, the timber wolf, which today is practically extinct except in the north. Since 1875 the United States Fish and Wildlife Service, empowered by an Act of Congress, has waged the greatest varmint war in history against it. Across the Great Plains coyotes have been shot, poisoned, trapped, gassed, run over and clubbed. In 1966 the retired chief biologist for the U.S. National Parks, Victor Cahalane, estimated the annual kill for the States and Canada at 125,000. By 1972 it was 200,000. In most years coyote pelts out-number even muskrat pelts in the North American fur trade. (And because poisons kill indiscriminately, there is a heavy toll of other meat- eaters like lynx, bobcat, fox, skunk, raccoon, badger, bear, cougar, eagle, condor.)

Yet the little wolf has continued to thrive. And, thanks to the ecology movement, what was once an almost pathological hatred among Americans toward coyotes seems to be softening. In 1972 President Nixon banned the use of poisons, but howls from the sheepmen led Ford to reinstate them three years later for limited use, with the proviso that $2.4 million (roughly a dollar for every coyote in the country) be put into research on selective controls.

Still, it will take time to undo a century of malice. In *Travels with Charley*, John Steinbeck tells how, when he came upon two coyotes out on the Mojave Desert, he instinctively reached for his rifle. After all, he told himself as he lined them up in his telescopic sights, didn't coyotes steal chickens and thin the ranks of quail? But when he had them in the crosshairs, "their little lemon-yellow eyes plainly visible," he could not pull the trigger. With their lives in his hands, he reminded himself that there wasn't a chicken within thirty miles and that the Mojave wasn't quail country. Steinbeck ended up leaving two opened cans of dog food "as a votive."

As coyotes increase in the Maritimes (or at least in New Brunswick and Nova Scotia; it's unlikely they will invade Prince Edward Island), so will conflict with people. Many who today view this new species as a natural curiosity and a good thing may change their minds. Our sheep industry is not that big, and its profit margin is not so ample that it can afford to lose more than a few per cent a year. Trappers in New Brunswick already complain that the coyote—even though its pelt fetches up to $75 and the animal can be legally trapped—will cut into the natural foods of such traditional fur bearers as fox, raccoon, fisher and bobcat. Maine deer hunters have been trying since 1973 to pass a bounty law that would slap a $50 price on the head of every coyote—even though coyotes seldom take any but aged or sick deer, and bounties are condemned by most wildlife administrators as both costly and futile.

Maybe we can learn from all this. Maybe we can start where Steinbeck left off. For in spite of its chicken-thief, lamb-killer image, the coyote is a handsome native dog that was here on this continent —at least in the West—long before Europeans arrived.

He may have lived in the East, too. In 1974 Frances L. Stewart of the Archeological Survey of Canada, probing Indian shell-heaps along New Brunswick's Passamaquoddy Bay, found coyote jawbones dating back three thousand years—enough pedigree for any dog. Plains Indians called it "God's Dog" and said it would be the last animal on earth. That should be ample warning to any politician contemplating easy votes.

A hundred years ago our great-grandfathers helped drive the eastern timber wolf to extinction. Now its smaller cousin has ventured to test our hospitality. It will be interesting to see how we respond. Personally, I'm looking forward to my first coyote serenade.

Any wolf is better than none.

—1978

• Caplin Scull •

L istening, a stranger would conclude it was a picnic, or else some sort of orgy connected with the first full moon of summer. Delighted squeals from women, gruff male shouts and peals of children's laughter come wafting up from the moonlit Newfoundland beach where dozens of people dart about knee-deep in the shallow sea water, dipping and scooping with nets and pails and even laundry baskets. The stranger would be mystified—until he scrambled down the rocky path to the beach and peering inside a pail saw the wriggling, silvery, smelt-like fish. In Norway or northern British Columbia he might see the same sight at about this time of year, for it's the annual visitation of that little northern fish—in our case *Mallotus villosus*, the caplin. Or, as they say in Newfoundland, "the caplin scull."

For millennia the caplin or capelin have been swarming onto northern beaches in late June or early July like this, usually in such unbelievable numbers that with any sort of container at all you can dip up hundreds in minutes. And what are the caplin up to? They are mating. More precisely, the females are laying their eggs while the males fertilize them with sperm-laden milt. Each female is escorted into shallow water by two males, one or her left and one on her right, each pressing against a special groove in her side until she releases her yellow spawn or eggs over the sandy bottom, where the tiny globes settle in their cloud of milt to incubate.

So it *is* an orgy of sorts, a love dance performed by iridescent silvery shapes shimmering in lilac and turquoise and brown along the green Atlantic strand. And the dance is orchestrated by the moon, whose position in relation to the sun at that time of year produces

our highest tides, the spring tides. Thus the caplin's eggs are laid as far up the beach as the sea ever comes except in storms. In that zone where—as any beachcomber knows—the water is warmest, they hatch in time for the next tides to bear them seaward. Meanwhile, their parents have retreated to deeper water to feed and rest before disappearing for another year.

In Newfoundland and Labrador the time of the caplin scull or school holds special meaning. Like the time of the gaspereau migration up Maritime rivers, it's a period of intense excitement for rural people of all ages. To the inshore cod fisherman it means a source of free bait. Moreover, it's a sign the cod have struck in, for the caplin is the cod's chief summer food until the squid arrive. Indeed, in Old Portuguese whence the name derives, it meant the 'cod fish', or literally 'the fish which the cod follows'. Ephraim Tucker said in 1839 that "there is no prey of which the cod seems to be so fond.... According to the plenty or scarcity of those capling [*sic*] do the fishermen prognosticate the result of their labours."

To a lesser extent it still means a source of nutritious human food as well. In former times it was rare for an outport family to be without a barrel of them dried and salted away for the winter plus a few bags for the dogs. The latter were apt to be lowgrade fish spoiled by untimely rains. Although the first caplin to hit the beaches are the fattest and sweetest, good drying weather is scarce in June around Newfoundland and Labrador. For this reason cool foggy days are often called 'caplin weather'. So people often had to re-salt and re-dry the maggot-chewed remnants of the first batch for the sled dogs, and catch some more for themselves.

In the days before bagged fertilizer, caplin also helped to grow fine crops of potatoes, turnips, cabbage and carrots. Although the tops of the potato leaves would be poking through the soil by the time the scull arrived, men and women would walk up and down the rows with a loaded dung bar (half a flour barrel fitted with pole handles) and scatter the little fish among the plants, after which they carefully hilled the potatoes. Although this buried the caplin, once July came on it was no trouble to tell they where there. As they gave up their nitrogen, phosphorus and above all calcium to the sour soil, the squeamish passerby had to concentrate his or her thoughts on what a power of good this monstrous stink was doing.

One of the most memorable sights of the caplin scull is that of cast-netting. The image of a man flinging a circular net, silhouetted against the sky, is surely one of those timeless icons of our dependence on Nature. To most it evokes a picture of southern climes, of Lake Titicaca in the Andes perhaps, or a Tahitian lagoon. Yet not so long ago it was a common sight in Newfoundland. The *Dictionary of Newfoundland English* defines a cast-net as "an open-mouthed, circular and weighted net thrown by hand among schooling caplin and drawn ashore or to the boat as the net is closed on the catch." Lead balls about three-fourths of an inch in diameter molded from sheet lead or tea chest lining were threaded around the skirt of this net, which opened to encompass a circle five or six feet wide as it fell. If the fish were schooling close to shore the fisherman would fling it where the water 'wrinkled' or where he could actually see them. If they were in deeper water he would judge their whereabouts by telltale bubbles dimpling the surface.

Says Aubrey Tizzard in his book *On Sloping Ground*: "The cast-net would be then thrown down and drawn up full of caplin, and this was tremendously hard work, pulling up a cast-net full of caplin in near forty feet of water." Still, success meant he had bait for another day or two. But to be a topnotch cast-netter took years of practice. Sometimes the price was a missing tooth. Like a cowboy's lariat, the net must form a circle in the air. To accomplish this the fisherman grasps the heavy skirt in both hands while holding a third part in his teeth. Biting on one of the lead weights, it's a simple thing to lose a tooth if he fails to let go at the right instant.

Food, bait and fertilizer—quite a role for one diminutive fish. Today, as in Tucker's time, inshore fishermen who appreciate its parallel role in the marine ecology watch its comings and goings with some trepidation. In recent years large quantities have been seined and sold to foreign interests who ship it back home for the fresh frozen market. Will such harvests, lucrative as they are for our fishermen, deplete the caplin—and with them the cod? Nobody really knows. Except among Newfoundlanders, caplin have never really caught on as a food fish here. Sometimes one sees them displayed in cellophane in the supermarkets, but they don't seem to sell very fast. Orientals are by far the most avid buyers.

This was brought home to me forcefully last summer while visiting an uncle in St. John's. Uncle Harry lives above the harbour entrance and one afternoon as we sat and talked, a bright red bulk carrier came slowly out through the Narrows escorted by tugs. At least five hundred feet long, it was well laden and low in the water. "What's she carrying?" I asked as we watched the ship glide beneath us.

"That one?" he said. "She's full of caplin for Japan."

Never had I imagined so many caplin in one place. How many sculls from how many beaches, I wondered, did it take? And how many shiploads like that would leave our shores that year? Only a week before I had heard concerns expressed on local television that the caplin stocks were being depleted.

Still, whatever the fate of the humble caplin, its place in the folklore of Newfoundland and Labrador is secure. Many place names owe their existence to it. The language is salted with such expressions as 'caplin weather', 'caplin trip' (a Grand Banks voyage using caplin for bait), 'caplin and lilacs' (which appear about the same time), and 'caplin-sick' (said of cod which have gorged on them and won't take bait). Caplin is called 'the poor man's food', and a bayman's sandwich is derisively defined as 'a caplin between two beach rocks'.

I once had a small painting of mine stolen from an art show in Halifax. The owner of the gallery was very upset. I felt secretly pleased. Imagine someone wanting a picture of mine badly enough to swipe it. I tried to guess what sort of a person it might have been. The scene was of caplin schooling near a sandy shore at dusk.

A homesick fellow Newfoundlander?

—1985

• Birdupmanship •

I suppose it's a sign of old age, but I'd rather look *back* on winter than look forward to it. Along about now, with the worst behind us and spring not quite a certainty, I like to recall the good parts and salt them away against summer's inevitable doldrums.

This winter, if we ignore its manifold fiscal and military alarms, has surely been an improvement over the last few. Lots of snow for a change...poor logging, but fine skiing and tobogganing...cozy times for the strawberry patch...frozen onions in the loft maybe, but fair skating on the meadow...hard on the woodpile, but easy on the oil barrel if you happen to have both.

One of the high points of the winter for us was the Advent of Birds at Our Feeder. I don't mean your everyday house sparrow or junco; I mean high class types. Now I'm no devotee of bird-watching. I'm not like a fellow I once knew who doffed his hat to ospreys overhead. But I do like the local birds to have a good opinion of me, especially in winter.

What I'm getting at is that it's hard to take when your friends keep dropping the names of exotic specimens who've come calling at *their* feeder, when the most colourful thing you've seen is a starling. When you have bought the right kind of seed and set up feeders of CMHC-approved design and kept the dog in at critical times, and they still don't come, what can a person conclude but that the birds don't like him?

So after exhausting the more conventional reasons—too many cats, bad location, land-clearing by our neighbours—I moved on to darker suspicions. Were we buying our feed at the wrong store? Was our rooster secretly running us down in his morning

pronouncements? Did the birds resent me for being a forester—
tree-killer, green blood on my hands...?

On a fine day like this, as I look out my window and admire the
sane spring sunshine thawing the dimpled snowbanks, I can laugh
it off. But at the time it seemed a serious matter. I took to sending
away for literature on better homes and gardens for birds; one spring
when I should have been rooting out couch grass I wheelbarrowed
home dozens of wild sapling cherry, mountain-ash, elderberry and
shadbush to make a hedge no bird could resist. I even found a source
in Maine for Russian olive; one winter I constructed a glassed-in
chalet for them, not to mention a clever clothesline-operated feeder
and a very attractive suet log.

The most I attracted was some miscellaneous sparrows.
Sparrows are okay (I said) if counting spots and eye-patches are your
thing. I was a little bitter.

Before my ardour cooled I established a kestrel box on a proper
pole, and projected robin nest platforms in my hedge. But it was all
baying at the moon. The cherries caught black knot, the elderberries
withered. My platforms never got built. Starlings took over the
kestrel hotel.

Bird-wise, the present winter started out no better. Having long
since abandoned hope I never even bothered to set up a feeder. A
few handfuls of the hens' scratch grain flung about the yard and that
was it.

Came a blizzard, a hard freeze, and yet another Christmastime.
And then it happened.

"Hey, Dad, Mom! Come see, come see! Some kind of partridge
I think...?"

We ran. Sure enough, darting about like windblown brown
leaves on the lawn, pecking at the bare green spots, was a covey of
Huns. Later, toward sunset on Christmas Eve, what should appear
but a flock of mourning doves, the first we had seen in eleven years
of living here. We knew them right off: that highbrowed pigeon look,
that neat tan and gray vesture with a hint of peacock iridescence, the
arrowy tail and fluttery wings. But we knew them only from books—
no way to know a bird. They reminded me of passenger pigeons,
their cousins now departed, whose millions we will never see again.

The next morning, while we are unwrapping presents and
munching hot cornbread, comes the cry, "Quick! Look at the
pheasants!"

Pheasants?!? Sure enough, down at the end of the lane we could see these three ringnecks, two hens and a cock, coming our way. Hesitantly at first, like children entering a strange playground, they advanced, mincing past the mailbox, peering into the clump of weathered artichokes, navigating gingerly between apple and plum tree, pausing often to scan the fortifications. Emboldened by hunger the cock forged ahead now and the hens followed, moving up our sloping lawn ("Quiet now, kids; they might hear us..."), nearer and nearer until the cock's scarlet mask glowed like a stop-light against the snow. And there they were, elegant in copper, tan and green, under our very eyes. Accustomed as we were to drab grays and browns, we were dazzled.

At one point on Boxing Day we counted at the feeder fourteen doves, three pheasants, eight or ten bluejays, a dozen juncos and as many sparrows (song, swamp and chipping), plus a starling and a grackle. A snow bunting dropped by too. There was even a chickadee —something we hadn't seen there in winter for years.

What, we wondered briefly, had we done to deserve such honour? But mostly we were too busy with the season and with putting out more feed and with shooing the dog indoors. Every day they came. Every day, that is, until Old Christmas Day. On that morning, January 6, we woke to find only sparrows and juncos under the lilac bush. The party was over. A mystery.

We felt let down. One day as I was slipping back into my old paranoia my wife said, "Wonder if the Guilds are back from Ontario yet?" Bob and Florence Guild are friends who live just up the road. They don't boast about it, but for years they have had the best of feathered company.

Like a flash it hit me: we were feeding second-hand birds. Brazen opportunists! When the Guilds' board went bare they'd switched allegiance overnight.... Two-timers!

Then my wife reminded me of how tough it is to be a bird in winter; and of how our good neighbours, with their alder thicket and brushy railway line and nearby woodlot, did after all enjoy a more birdy location. Clearly, if G & B's Diner expected to lure customers away from Chez Guild, we'd have to try harder.

Yessir, as soon as these snowbanks are gone I'm going to turn this half-acre into a winter sanctuary. Then next Yuletide season, when the Guilds go visiting and their feeder is cleaned out, I'll throw my gala opening. Even the chickens will be invited. I'll be hobnobbing with evening grosbeaks and purple finches yet, even if I have to steal them. Or I'll be a raven's uncle.

—1981

A Simpler Time

Take me back to that snug green cove
Where the seas roll up their thunder.

Otto P. Kelland
"Let Me Fish Off Cape St. Mary's"
(Newfoundland Folk Song)

• Killicks •

The rotund tourist chuckled so hard that he nearly fell backwards off the stagehead. "A wooden anchor, did you say? Oh, come now! I'm not as green as all that, you know!"

"Well, we might as well call it that, mightn't we?" returned the fisherman with a grin. "For look: the most of it is made of plain, ordinary spruce; take away the rock and your killick is a wooden anchor, isn't it?"

"The what?"

"Killick. Some says kellick, but 'tis all the same. Just a home-made graplin, that's all."

"Graplin? I'm afraid you're losing me. You Newfoundlanders...."

"Well, I believe 'grapnel' is Mr. Webster's word for it, sir; but I think ours sounds more better, somehow."

And somehow the stone-weighted killick *looks* more better than a store-bought iron grapnel—in the same way that the hand-sewn birch bark canoe had more character, if you will, than the latest fiberglass car-topper. Not that the old things did the job any better. Any Iroquois brave, for instance, might have been delighted to get his hands on a modern archery outfit. The charm, I suppose, lies in the clear imprint of the human hand and mind upon these cruder implements, an imprint which the gloss of mechanical surfaces seems to conceal.

The killick used today by East Coast fishermen is the second oldest anchor in the world. The oldest was a pierced stone used by ancient seafaring peoples like the Phoenicians, who also used bags filled with stones or sand. The third oldest was the Roman anchor with lead-filled wooden shaft used in Christ's day, prototype of the traditional anchor shape as seen on *Popeye's* arm. Somewhere between Phoenician and Roman times, then, the anchor we call a killick evolved. A closer fix on its origin is difficult. Old killicks disintegrate into indistinguishable sticks and stones. Few if any relics remain—except those in day-to-day use in Newfoundland and parts of Nova Scotia. Judging by the extreme simplicity of construction, however,the killick of 1963 differs little from that of 100 B.C.

To make one, take four small, dry spruce or juniper rods, two short flat boards, an oval stone, and some stout twine. The weight you want will dictate the size of these parts. Cross-fasten the boards firmly at their midpoints and at right-angles. Bore four holes, one in each arm, to take the rods snugly. Now, insert the rods small end first and jam them tight. Saw off the excess. Then, into the cage thus made drop a stone too big to slip out. Gather the rod-ends and bind them with twine. Finally, sharpen the boards for a better grip, fasten a rope where the rods are tied. You have your killick.

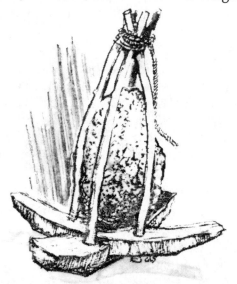

Cost? Well, if you cut the wood yourself and used home-made leather lashings—nothing. Yet your creation would serve to moor boats and anchor nets as well as the blacksmith's article, because it would be heavy, grip the bottom well, and resist rolling. And when the rods 'plimmed up' or swelled with moisture, they wouldn't work loose.

Blacksmiths and money were scarce on the East Coast in the early days. Why travel thirty miles and lose a day's pay to buy a thing one could make for oneself? So, drawing on the ancient lore of his West Country and Channel Islands ancestors—who in turn probably drew theirs from yet more ancient Mediterranean lore—he took the materials at hand and fashioned the thing he needed. The term 'killick' or 'kellick' came naturally, since it was and is a name used among English-speaking sailors to describe a small anchor.

The best place to look for killicks in Newfoundland (apart from the curio shops, where small replicas are sold for paperweights) is any place where herring or salmon are netted. Both fish frequent relatively shallow waters where the great holding power of big iron grapnels is not needed. Two serve to keep each net in place. In winter, if the net site is far from home, many fishermen leave these anchors on the beach nearby. They won't rust, and nobody wants to steal a killick. At any rate, nobody used to....

Apart from the standard killick described, which weighs on the average about thirty pounds, a lighter and simpler version is made. It has only two rods set in a single cross-piece, and holds a flat stone instead of an oval stone. The flat stone, because it resists rolling and causes one of the blades to dig in, takes the place of the extra cross-piece in the common type. This form of anchor is encountered where shale and other types of stratified rock are more abundant than chunky types such as granite.

There is also a heavy-duty killick. It takes two men to carry some of these, and since the heaviest are all but impossible to lift over the gunwale of a boat at sea, an ingenious trip-string device is incorporated in the design, allowing the rock to be released and the frame to be retrieved with ease.

And many queer hybrids exist. Often one sees oak barrel staves instead of native spruce or fir in the blades, and scrap iron in place of a stone. One man from Gander Bay conceived what he thought to be a more efficient model by reversing the bevelling of the blades and tying his rope to the head instead of the handle. It worked fine.

The killick will likely continue unaltered into the Space Age, along with grub-hoes, grasshooks, moldboard plows and all such wonderful implements from a simpler time.

—1963

• Voyage to the Ice •

You slept in a cramped wooden bunk with a side board so you wouldn't fall out when the ship rolled. Your dreams were dreamt to the growl of ice and the swash of sea-water six inches from your ear. At dawn most days you ate beans or scones washed down with strong tea, then joined your watch crew on deck while the steamer nosed its way into the prairie of ice pans. The ice was dotted with gray harp seals and their white pups. Over this vast nursery there rose a sound like the murmer of a thousand well-fed human babies and the soughing of a thousand pine trees. Everything—the ship, the ice, the seals, the clouds—was in slow motion.

While waiting for the ship to halt you looked to your gear: stout gaff armed with a boathook for clubbing the seals and for jumping pans, and saving yourself if you fell in; a coil of manila rope carried slantwise across your chest for hauling pelts together in piles; razor-sharp sculping knife for peeling the pelts off with their thick layer of fat; plenty of pointed ice-nails or sparables in your boots, and snow goggles if you were lucky enough to own a pair.

"Now, b'ys!" your Master Watch would yell, and over the rail you went then and down the wooden ladders lashed to her rusty sides, remembering to jump well clear at the waterline so you wouldn't fall between the ship and the grinding pans.

Soon the old steamer would be only a smudge of black smoke on the skyline, leaving you and your mates right where you wished to be—alone on the heaving icefloes, miles from land, surrounded by fifty thousand seals.

Then all day long, stopping only long enough to gnaw your hardtack, you'd run and club and skin and jump from pan to pan and haul and pile. Sometime before dark the ship would return. A quick supper on board, then it would be hoist and stow till midnight or later, and finally a mug-up, and you'd fall dog-tired into the blessed bunk.

But should a blizzard find you before the captain could, or should the wind veer offshore and drive the floes apart…then you might well join the ghosts of hundreds of dead who'd sailed on the *Greenland*, the *Newfoundland*, the *Viking* and others….

Thoughts like these must have filled the mind of Michael Kieley of Holyrood, a thirty-year-old carpenter with a wife and two sons, as he boarded the evening train for St.John's that spring in 1940 to sign up for his first voyage to the ice. Only a week before he'd all but given up hope. He knew that for every available berth there would be five or ten men like himself eager for the chance to go. For years the catch had been falling off, and now there was this ugly U-boat war to scare the merchant outfitters into safer ventures. Yet the phone call had come. Bowring Brothers Limited had offered him a berth. His ship would be the S.S. *Beothic*, built in 1918 at Lorain, Ohio, total tonnage 1,825, Wilfred Barbour the captain.

He could see it all now. Down the harbour she would steam, parading single file with other veterans like the *Eagle* and the *Ungava* and the *Imogene*, rainbow flags snapping from all stays and shrouds, whistles echoing off the South Side hills, crews crowding the taffrails to wave and wave to loved ones and well-wishers—some of whom would linger till the last stern faded out the Narrows in a squall of snow.

As sealing voyages go, Mike Kieley's first trip to the ice was nothing exceptional. The ship wasn't stove in or sunk. No one was lost. The catch was fair. All hands made some money. But one thing about it was remarkable: Kieley kept a diary. Few who went to the ice ever did this. Most couldn't write. Those with enough education to do so were usually too nice in themselves to bloody their boots and were content to watch from the safety of the deck.

Not Kieley. To my mind his words, pencilled into a writing pad in dim light after numbing toil or during slack spells, say more about sealing than either the coffee-table sagas of disaster or the rhetoric of well-meaning environmentalists who can't see the men for the seals:

March 9: Steaming through heavy slob ice all afternoon, ESE of Cape Bauld. Got our gaff and hauling rope all ready, sharpened our knives, *Neptune* and *Ungava* in company. Enjoyed the day watching her steaming through ice. Rice and prunes for supper.

March 10: Up and to breakfast of fish and brewis; blowing from SE, got in slob ice and making slow progress. No sign of seals yet.

March 13: Got up steam at daylight. Was standing on deck when the captain sang out: "Boys, get ready; the *Imogene* is putting her men out!" Well now, that was excitement: every man getting ready their lunch bags, gaffs and ropes, etc. She steamed along slow and our watch was the first called to go over her side and down the side-sticks. Believe me, I wasn't far behind Billy, our Master Watch. She drops off four men at a time as we go along. Billy sculps a whitecoat and I look to see how it's done. Nothing to it. The first one I bat is an old one and I sculp it OK. We work together all morning. Later, she steams along the pan and four or five men get down and strap on; at this all afternoon. On watch then, 5 to 8 p.m. Had mug-up and then to bed. Our total kill today is 8,000, took 2,000 on board. The ice is very bad with a heavy swell and you have to be like the cat to get around. One of the crew had his finger nearly bitten off by an old seal.

March 19: Very stormy this morning, wind from NE; cleared up a little after breakfast. Overboard at 8:30 a.m. We take flags and go look for some to kill. Only 28 men in our watch today, all the rest ice-blind. Billy in today; his eyes are very sore. We travelled for three hours and run across whitecoats fairly plenty. We must kill about 800. I sculped 26 for my share. They are large size now. Got aboard 6 p.m., had flippers for supper. Feel eyes a little sore.

March 21: The ice opened up a lot today so we had a hard travel back to ship. We did good work picking up pans and took aboard 5,000. Beautiful sunshiny day, wind NW, the best day we had this spring. Billy and I felt our eyes very sore last night, so we put raw potatoes to them; cured them OK. Never missed a day so far, T.G. To bed at 8:30 p.m. Winches still going hoisting in seals.

March 22, Good Friday: Think everyone feeling in good humour now that we have most of the fat on board.

March 24, Easter Sunday: Up at 5:30. On watch about ten minutes when she burned down for the night. All glad to get below—bitter cold. Had nice cup hot cocoa, then down aft to the Rosary. A lot of pans missing—must be stolen. Must have killed about 30,000, will only get 20,000—a big loss.

March 26: *Eagle* came alongside, transferred man very sick with pneumonia aboard. Doctor treating him back aft in the hospital.

April 2: All hands on deck, gunners and dogs went ahead and started killing the bedlamers; fifteen minutes later, every man went over the side and followed the gunners, sculping and panning what was shot. Well, what a racket: you'd think it was a battlefield, nothing but *Crack! Crack!* It was a good patch of seals. The gunners account for 3,000 today. Took a lot aboard and have torches on every pan. Still picking up pans—be at it all night.

April 3: Up and to breakfast at 4 a.m., over her side after daylight. Snowing thick till 9 a.m. Went and sculped what was left since yesterday, cleaned them all up and got aboard at 11:30 a.m.. Ice went apart bad, and had hard going to get aboard. Three hours sleep. Went on watch 5 p.m., stowing seals aft. Reported we will be going home Friday or Saturday, also reported that young fat is gone up 25 a quintal; so every little is a help. George T. from Broad Cove got a message that his wife and baby were dead; a hard blow and he is thinking hard of it, poor fellow. The sick man off the *Eagle* is improving.

April 5: Decided to go aft to the Doctor and get out the tooth that bothered me. When he got it out it was the wrong one—my wisdom tooth. On the second try he got the right one. Great talks of us going in port tomorrow.

April 9: Taking ice aboard for water tank. Seals very wild; over 2,000 today, and got most of them on board. Master Watch fell in, escaped.

April 10: Ice bad. Some of our men out in dory, worked all evening getting more ice for water tank. The line parted from the pan we were on and we had to hustle aboard. *Neptune's* crew shared $31.96.

April 12: War news very serious.

April 14: The time seems wonderful long to us all now....

April 15: Everything covered with sleet. Uncle Bob telling yarns tonight.

April 16: Have close to 30,000. Only 3,000 shells left, so if we get a run out tomorrow we will use them up, we might go home then.

April 17: Miserable day, blowing hard with wet snow. It seems a year since we left.

April 18: Fellows on deck beating ice from rigging woke us at 5 a.m.

April 19: Working old seals near French Shore and Cape Bauld. Young M. fell down by side of ship trying to get on side-sticks; escaped without a wetting. And now I have the best Bit of News I wrote since we came out: she is bore up for home, steaming S by W. Well now, you might say everybody is merry aboard tonight. Will and I have a dozen flippers to bring home. Watch crew lowering derrick, getting ready for the rough-and-tumble. She is rolling like a cradle now, and I guess she will do something more before the night is out as there is a SE storm predicted. The wind is freshening now, 10 p.m. Uncle Bob made us a mug of ginger wine, Sam M. gave us a few jigs on the mouth organ, and as usual Ed C. put on his queer act.

April 20: Slept as sound as a rock last night. Beautiful morning, sun shining and getting warmer as we go south. Steaming full speed, no ice and very smooth. Passed Funks at 11 a.m. Worked an hour washing down deck. Passed Cabot Islands at 3 p.m.—a lovely sight. They signalled with their flag; we signalled back with ours and three blows of our whistle. Could see the men and women plainly, waving their hands, and saw one fellow throw his cap up in the air. Everybody cleaning up this evening. Gave in our ropes and gaffs. Most of us getting short of tobacco. Passed Cape Bonavista and 26 miles now to Baccalieu and 36 from there to St.John's. Lovely night, stars shining, bit cold. Ed C. went wild altogether—worse night he was since we came out. They woke everyone up.

April 21, Sunday: (Anchored in stream, St.John's). Up at 5 a.m., all crew on deck passing Torbay. Smooth as a pond once we get inside the Narrows. Dropped anchor. Awaiting harbour Doctor: no one allowed ashore until then. This concludes my Diary of the Voyage and I might say I enjoyed it. It was all new to me and I think it's a great sport. The crew are all the finest kind, and sure for the men who bunked near Will and me you could not meet better. The voyage is a fairly good one too: we hail for 30,000 and expect to turn out 32,000. We should make $60 or $65 apiece. Doctor just came aboard—8 a.m. Will and I ready to go ashore and see if we can get home.

—1978

Note: The *Beothic* was lost off northeast Newfoundland in the fall of 1940, running freight to Labrador.

• Ample Width and Proper Fulness •

You know how it is when a tree you've known since childhood falls down and leaves a hole in the sky. Silly as it sounds, that's how I felt for a while when I heard in January 1976 that Eaton's mail order catalogue was to be discontinued. The feeling caught me by surprise. Nostalgia for its own sake bores me; talk of the Good Old Days turns me off. And of course I knew there were still plenty other catalogues around: Sears, Canadian Tire, Buildall.... For that matter, we hadn't ordered from Eaton's twice in five years. If the company had lost $17 million on its catalogue sales in 1975 as it claimed, I suppose we were part of their problem.

The reason for my twinge of sentiment lay in my childhood. We grew up with The Catalogue. So did our parents and grandparents. It was the only one we knew. To us it seemed as permanent as the friendly hills and as dependable as the seasons. Didn't the *Spring and Summer* issue appear about the time the ice went out of the ponds? And the *Fall and Winter* when the maples and birches were turning red and gold? We grew up thinking it would last forever.

It almost did. The first edition came out in 1844—a long life for any publication. But Kenneth Ferguson, a crusty Scottish settler who witnessed its arrival in Cape Breton Island, would have throttled it at birth. Alarmed at its growing popularity among the women, he railed:

> It wasn't Eaton's we depended on to keep us supplied with clothing, but industrious mothers with their knitting needles in winter. But that time has gone, and it won't return, and probably the world isn't growing any better—an impetuous world in a frenzy for finery, and the women tired out with dancing.

Kenneth, thou shouldst be living at this hour!

Yet I suppose he had a point. The influx of factory-made, Upper Canadian goods was indeed a threat to the self-reliant life Down East settlers had known. Along with the railroads that followed, perhaps this first incursion of the Toronto adman's art did in a small way help silence the spinning wheel and the smithy.

We felt differently than Ferguson. To us, living in the 1940s in an isolated Newfoundland community serviced only by coastal steamer and river boat, the catalogue was our only big store. For two generations or more it had served the people well. They trusted Eaton's to deliver the goods. When Eaton's declared (as they did in the 1901 issue) that "There is nothing mean or skimped in this lot of Petticoats, they have ample width and proper fullness," the matron of the house could depend on it. "As nice as anything you'd see in Eaton's" became a synonym for quality.

Besides, each new catalogue was a sort of education—like finding an up-to-date encyclopedia after years on a desert island. Armed with *The Toronto Star Weekly*, *The Family Herald* and Eaton's latest catalogue, one could form a tolerably accurate idea of what the outside world was up to. At least so far as vital issues like Superman's latest exploits or the newest Toronto fashions were concerned. That was how we youngsters felt. For our elders it was probably different.

I can feel the heft of the *Fall and Winter* now as I hurry home from the post office clutching the floppy manila-wrapped slab. And as we break into it and finger the cool smooth pages I can smell the tarry-piney fragrance of ink and newsprint.

Eagerly the boys would thumb their way to the gleaming harmonicas from M. Hohner, Germany, the sleek air rifles by Daisy, the woolly red-checked mackinaws guaranteed to keep you snug in the worst blizzard or your money cheerfully refunded. Just as eagerly, the girls would hurry to get a look at the latest 'Eaton's Beauty' doll or the new hats and high-heeled shoes.

For weeks this window-shopping would go on. But soon more weighty matters were at hand. Winter was imminent. Even though all our mitts and most of our sweaters were still home-made, boots and jackets and underwear had to be ordered. Ordering was a job for the level heads of mothers. For new garments there were sessions with measuring tape ("Stand still, I said!"), and for footwear she would make pencil tracings of our feet ("Stop wiggling those toes!"). Finally, when all the proper codes had been inserted in the proper boxes on the order form, all the prices tallied up in pencil, a few items stroked off for economy, and the grand total inked in, the fateful envelope was on its way.

Few things in adult life have quite matched for me the delicious suspense that hummed in the air while we awaited the next mail. Weeks dragged like years. At last The Parcel would arrive, bulky in brown paper as the postmaster swung it through the wicket by its hemp twine, the outside all plastered with triangular labels spelling 'The T. EATON CO. Limited' in familiar block letters. "Now watch you don't lose the pink slips inside!" Mother would cry as she snipped the twine and we, like chickens jostling for a handful of grain, dived in and made the paper fly.

Inside, magically transformed from picture to reality and perfumed faintly with moth balls, would be the things we ordered—or reasonable substitutes. Often the grade of substitutes surpassed the things ordered. If not, Mother had the pink slips.

Each catalogue had to last six months till the new one came. Then the dog-eared survivor of half a year's pawing and poring might be released from duty and given to us to use as we wished. Talk about recycling paper. Eaton's customers invented it—or at least their own version. Catalogues were never thrown out. It reminds me of a Hungarian immigrant's telling me how he and his family could not get over the largesse of bottles and jars in this country, and only gave up trying to save them all when their small apartment overflowed. We were like that with catalogues—except that we managed to keep ahead of them.

On stormy days girls would sit crosslegged by the hour, snipping out female models and pieces of apparel and matching them in complex and endless arrangements on the floor, until the pages of the ladies' wear section were tattered and impossible to turn. Sometimes nervous giggles would ripple among them as they paused to stare at the trusses and pessaries and other unmentionables displayed on certain pages.

Meanwhile, their brothers would abscond with whole sections to pad their bony shins in hockey games. Fifty pages wadded inside a thick home-knit sock could absorb quite a whack. Sometimes the boys too would stop to gape at certain other pages, especially the ones where brassieres and corsets barely concealed swelling bosoms and buttocks.

Any catalogues which avoided these indignities and escaped the wood stove came at last to the outhouse, the end of the line. Compared to the soft red or white tissue wrappers off Christmas oranges and apples, the smooth catalogue paper was definitely inferior stuff. Even *The Family Herald* rated higher. But catalogue paper was abundant and dependable, whereas fruit wrappers were at best a seasonal luxury. Anyway, *The Family Herald* and *Star Weekly* were needed for cleaning sooty lamp chimneys and lighting fires.

The human body is a marvel of adaptability. By the time one got past the middle of the book and moved into the sections on farm machinery and water pumps, one hardly winced anymore. But the admen wanted colour printing. That meant slicker paper. At last even the hardiest had to embrace toilet tissue and indoor plumbing.

Who knows? Perhaps that was the beginning of the end for The Catalogue as an institution. Conveniences have a way of multiplying. One advance led to another, until finally the zenith of all convenience appeared: the all-weather shopping mall with ample parking. And what is that but a walk-in catalogue without the wait?

Or the magic, unfortunately.

—1977

• Truly a Different Matter •

Today, on schedule, the Co-op oil truck appears in my driveway. Alighting briskly, for he has many calls to make, the genial driver unreels his snakelike hose and sends another transfusion of furnace fuel coursing into our basement tank. Minutes later the snake has recoiled itself and the oilman roars off, leaving the company bill flapping in the door jamb. No fuss, no bother.

It made me muse on two other household heating fuels.

When I was eleven, living in St. John's, it was coal. "Son, it's that time again. Here's the scuttle." I despised that chore: lifting the heavy hatch at the foot of the stairs; descending into the black bin with the rackety, lop-sided bucket; groping for the lone forty-watt bulb; shovelling while the gritty dust stung my eyes and nose; scrambling up again with the awkward load barking my shins and mashing my knuckles. And somehow, among all those glistening lumps of coal, I never found a fossil fern or dragonfly print to brighten my toil.

The only good memory I have of coal is the coal man. Clattering down our street he would come in his grimy red cart, clucking to his horse and bantering in his Irish brogue as he backed the cart around and avalanched the black rocks into our cellar with a wonderful din.

Wood was truly a different matter. Of course—to be really honest about it—I didn't always relish my woodshed and woodbox chores either. Some of my affection stems from mere nostalgia. (But I don't admit this to my kids; so many nice theories of child-rearing venerate these objects that some of them just may be true.) Yet nostalgia can't account for the warmth I feel for firewood.

Spruce, fir and birch were our standbys, because the Maritimes' traditional rock maple and beech don't grow in Newfoundland. Even soft maple is scarce. So the softwoods had to be our main heating fuels, with white birch relied on for overnight stoking and to provide steady heat for baking.

Not much inferior to maple when properly dried, birch was a beautiful fuelwood in every way. It was easy to cut and handle, came pre-wrapped in its own tinder, and was fragrant in the stove.

Softwoods were troublesome and gave less heat. If at all green, they distilled brown creosote that ate out the stovepipes before their time and spattered the wallpaper to my mother's disgust. Fir, though aromatic, left sticky resin smears on hands and clothes. Spruce bark was flaky, and each armload littered the floors.

However, these were housewive's concerns and didn't trouble young boys. Besides, sometimes the spruce junks yielded jawbreaking knobs of frankgum that chewed out to a nice pink, leaving your teeth squeaky clean. And sometimes we got to hitch rides on the sleds or the horses, and even to roast caplin and brew tea over a midday campfire with the men in the woods.

Depending on how hard the winter, it took twelve to fifteen cords of wood to keep us warm. This all had to be felled, hauled, sawed, seasoned, split, piled and stowed, then fed to woodbox and stove—tactile experience enough to satisfy any educator! Not to mention the spin-off in elementary botany, physics, chemistry, animal husbandry, and meteorology. By late fall we usually had the woodshed bulging with summer-dried wood from the previous winter's cutting. As winter closed in on us, this affluence gave a feeling of security that somehow I haven't quite matched since, even with Canada Savings Bonds.

I'm sure our elders saw the whole thing much less romantically. My own initiation into the hard labour of felling and hauling was postponed when we moved to town. Moreover, I didn't have to clean the stove-pipes or sweep up the bark or worry over the constant menace of fire in the night. My parents were probably very relieved when we went to St.John's and switched to coal, and even more so when they got oil heat.

Still, it was they who told us: "Wood warms you twice; once in the chopping and once in the stove." Had they truly despised it they could have said worse. The saying has the ring of Robert Frost—who favoured wood.

There's a principle here somewhere. It must have to do with involvement. From stump to stove, firewood is all involvement. Coal is less so. And oil, though in one form or another it virtually sustains our society, is by nature remote, a cold colourless smelly liquid that is slippery and repulsive to the touch and poisonous to the body. It means almost nothing to me. I can't dig it or grow it. There's no local lore in it to teach my children, no rich tapestry of experience to bequeath. All I can do is pay the oilman's bill—whether he be the Co-op or King Faisal.

By paying it, however, I buy time and freedom that my father and forebears never had for doing things they might have liked to do; things which may free our generation to weave another kind of tapestry. By and large it's been a pretty good bargain. But lately, watching the price of milk rise whenever the Arab sheiks shrug or frown, I've begun to wonder. I've begun to comprehend how an old Micmac might have felt, paddling home from the trading post with a mess of beads and pots and whiskey for his canoe-load of rich pelts.

—1975

• Shopping Mall Blues •

Big indoor shopping malls turn me off. This troubles me sometimes, because most people seem to enjoy them. Being against them seems somehow unsociable, un-Canadian, even un-American.

But I can't help it. No sooner have I navigated the automatic doors than I am seized with moribund thoughts. Even before I reach the smiling fiberglass elephant that will give your kids a ride for a dime, a cloud of oppression has settled around my shoulders. By the time I pass the lifelike plastic philodendron in its pot of vermiculite I know the expedition will end badly.

I mean no offense. After all, the Indoor Shopping Mall with Ample Parking is a North American institution. A whole generation of shoppers will soon know no other way. It's only right that Atlantic Canadians should enjoy what Montrealers and Torontonians and Vancouverites have long taken for granted. Within the mall's gleaming portals at least, regional disparity seems to melt away. And even if the architecture—a blend of warmed-over Gropius and not-quite-Wright—can get to look monotonous and contrived, the weather inside is certainly an improvement over the real thing.

But I fear it's all wasted on the likes of me. The sight of all those antiseptic vistas makes me hanker for some muddy footprints. The rubber music soon grates on my nerves, the racket of cash registers shivers my ear drums. Among the pastel glades of ladies' undergarments and the dark forests of Levi cords I lose my way. Confronted with a wall of colour television sets all tuned to the same channel and all flickering the same image in surreal technicolour, I find my eye-blink rate accelerating to dangerous levels. Even the bright bins of tomatoes and grapes and cabbages, so pleasant to contemplate in roadside stands or at the corner grocery, seem somehow vulgar in their profusion and display, like a mouth-watering chocolate cake-mix television commercial after a CARE appeal from India.

From experience I know that a half hour of this is about my limit. I try to conduct my business within that span; if detained further I seek asylum in the pet corner. There, behind the shelves of bargain paints and pretend plug-in fireplaces I find solace in the company of cheerful budgerigars and dignified guppies. They are nonchalant. They have important matters to attend to. I like their style.

And this bit of Nature, however artificial or exotic, is usually all it takes to repair my composure and restore my perspective. Then I can recognize the reasons for my aversion. One is simply a distaste for the notion that Bigger is Better—the Brontosaurus Principle. This may be a good principle as long as energy is abundant and cheap. Then perhaps society can afford giant stores that are lavishly lit, heated and cooled by oil-based energy and which are patronized almost solely by motorized customers. But let energy grow scarce and dear, and your Brontosaurus is in trouble.

Another source of disaffection is my faith in the unpredictable. In a genuine small shop there is always a certain delicious uncertainty. One can Poke Around. In contrast, the average shopping mall—by cramming a grab-bag of different shops with familiar and often shoddy goods under one roof, all in the name of convenience and efficiency—only succeeds in destroying this, the very spice of happy shopping. Boil everything in the one pot and you get...stew. Stew is nice, but not as a steady diet.

A third objection stems from what seems to me a wanton use of land. To sprawl over as many acres as possible appears to be a point of honour with these developers. Their urban counterparts can't afford such one-storey extravanzas; their only vacant space is up. Stairs and escalators do not offend them. They seem to manage. Not so in the suburbs. Unfortunately, the elimination of climbing also means the elimination of productive woodland and farmland and marshland.

Woodland we still have plenty of—though the day is fast approaching when we'll wish we had more. Good farmland we have much less of—and the day has already come when woodland is again cleared for crops. In those instances we are at least making a conscious trade between forestry and agriculture. But when we seal good land under asphalt and brick we sacrifice future wood and food for mere shopping convenience. And already, as land values escalate, we are finding this trade-off harder to rationalize. More and more we are turning to so-called wasteland—such as marshes. Even then, nearby farmland and forest must be gouged and scarred to find the fill to raise the floors and parking lots above the water line. So far we seem to find this compromise acceptable. After all, it's only marsh....

Not to be maudlin or impractical; but is this really wise land use? More enlightened observers than I are convinced otherwise. They claim that the typical freshwater marsh is an unexcelled reservoir of rainfall. They say that it sponges up the cloudbursts and drizzles to release them later in such a way as to prevent downstream flooding or drought. They even state that in terms of total biomass of plant and animal life, marshland out-produces the best farmland. And they have proved that it stores and releases nutrients to enrich our streams and lakes for trout and bass and perch, and our estuaries which are nurseries for marine life. Knowing such things, are we wise to sink our marshland capital in such doubtful enterprises?

I am prejudiced, I know. I once watched such a marsh being erased to build a mall. Who demanded the mall I don't know. No petition was circulated. Maybe some anxious aldermen needed more tax money. Perhaps some worried merchants saw dollars whizzing past their town on the new highway. Anyway, one day trucks loaded with red gravel began to converge on the marsh. Bulldozers and builders followed. They worked day and night. It took a long time— but only seconds on the Pleistocene time-scale of the ancient marsh. At last the paving was done, the lamp-posts in place, the signs up, the arcades finished. A new shiny emporium turned on its lights and threw its opening sale.

Two years later the competition opened an even bigger emporium down the road on the same marsh. Swiftly the inevitable string of gas stations, car-washes, trailer marts and hamburger take-outs filled the gap between. Soon a lovely marsh lay silent under tile and asphalt, feet and wheels, and what was left of it disappeared behind storefronts and neon signs.

So now, when I loiter amid the chatter and warbling of budgies and canaries in any mall, my mind returns to a cloudless May morning when I stood in knee rubbers on that marsh, enjoying the rusty-hinge *konkaree* notes of red-winged blackbirds nesting in a green tangle of cattail rushes. The red-wing is a bird of some distinction—for a blackbird. The male sports startlingly vivid scarlet epaulets edged with lemon yellow. Most people have noticed the red; few have seen the yellow. Flashing like fire among the emerald cattails, these shoulder patches signal proprietorship.

Still loitering in the pet corner, I muse too on the sturdy cattails themselves: the pale green spring shoots that rival Swiss chard in succulence, the cigar-shaped flower heads loaded with green pollen, the starchy roots that can yield fifty times more flour per acre than wheat (flour with more protein and minerals than corn or rice)—as muskrats know well. The Indians feasted off cattails, and wove rush mats from the fronds. So did our forefathers.

And I think of the marsh in winter, when muskrat lodges dotted the far ice like miniature beaver houses, and thin snowdrifts embroidered the dead rustling forests of sedge and rush in mackerel patterns, with here and there a notation of mink tracks.

And the spring peepers, soul of the marsh. Robins are fine songsters to be sure, and passing fair to view on a broad green sward. But nothing so thrills the winter-weary Maritimer as the first tremulous flutings of the peepers. Listen at dusk some April evening. Tentatively at first, then swelling with certitude as more definite news of spring filters in from the cosmos, the trilling of these gherkin-sized musicians charms winter away. And the only pit this orchestra requires is an ordinary swamp.

Standing now at a checkout under an acre of hard white lights in the supermarket that usurped their singing grounds, I consider these things. As the harried cashier rings in our groceries I try to reckon things less tangible; mall against marsh, convenience against wilderness, profit against loss. But my books will not balance. On the way out I scan the cinema playbills for some redeeming note.

NOW PLAYING

The Arena—See Wild Women Fight to the Death

NEXT ATTRACTION

Rollerball

COMING SOON

Chain Saw Massacre

Outside in the cool night air, it happens to be spring. "Is this," I ask the peepers, "what we buried you for?" They make no reply.

—*1976*

• From Forest to Farm to Forest •

The pioneers would turn over in their graves if they knew. We've been letting their fields go back to forest—and we've been doing it for a good hundred years now. Anyone who travels our Maritime country roads has seen it: the weathered house and barn reeling at drunken angles, the apple orchard tottering on its last legs, the rail fence drowning in goldenrod, the fields pocked with spruce and alders. Where once axes rang and teamsters shouted and women crooned over babies and children laughed and cattle stirred in their stalls at dawn and the smoke of breakfast fires ascended, now only the hooting of owls breaks the midnight silence and only a tatter of crows greets the sunrise.

I find it sad.

There are sound economic reasons for this dereliction, I know. But I also know that neat theories do not begin to measure the toil, the sheer human effort, that went into clearing the wilderness in those days before power chain saws and bulldozers and easy government aid.

> Many a labour I'll be involved in before I can make my living secure; my work will be exhausting before I get any returns from it and before I make a clearing for the plough. Piling tree-trunks on top of each other in bonfires has strained every muscle in my back, and every part of me is so black that I'm just like a chimney-sweep. Before I make a clearing and raise crops I'll be worn out, and almost spent before my children have grown up.

So wrote Nova Scotia's Gaelic bard John MacLean in his rueful "Song to America." MacLean came from Scotland in the early 1800s and settled at Barney's River near Antigonish, a region of rolling hardwood hills and dark evergreen intervales where autumn frosts strike early and winter snows linger late.

Not all our pioneers were so pessimistic. But all of them worked hard and all suffered privation. After the harrowing ocean voyage from Britain or Europe most of them faced a sombre prospect where roads were rare, doctors even rarer, and medicines mostly home-made; where unaccustomed cold and heat and biting insects assailed them and suitable clothing had to be devised from local materials; where lifelines to the mother country or loved ones were long and tenuous and often severed by war; where the natives were often unfriendly.

And always the sombre wilderness stared in at their windows. Margaret Atwood put it well:

The house pitched
the plot staked
in the middle of nowhere
In the darkness the fields
defend themselves with fences
   everything
   is getting in.

Above all they hated the forest. Though it fed and sheltered them, it was the greatest obstacle to settlement and mocked their puny efforts. For they faced not a spindly second-growth pulpwood forest such as we mostly see today; they faced the great trees of the forest primaeval.

Anyone who has felled a maple two or three feet in diameter with only an axe knows how much labour it takes. And that was only the first step. For every acre wrested from the forest hundreds of trees had to be felled, limbed, junked, piled and burned. In the spring and fall acrid smoke filled the clearings day and night. Then the ashes had to be spread so that potatoes and other crops could be planted among the stumps. Only later, when the stumps had either rotted away or been pulled out, could the land be properly plowed and sown.

The Acadian settlers chose not to clear much woodland, but to win their acres from the sea. They too toiled incessantly in the early years, fighting the tides to build eight-foot dykes of timber and mud to wall out the sea from the fertile salt marshes, and building their ingenious aboîteaux so the brooks could run out without letting the sea in. If we consider the two or three fallow years required to flush the salt from such newly drained land, it is clear that the Acadians had no magic land-making formula either.

Thousands of settlers quit. Some returned home. Most took off for the less demanding life of town or city. But others, perhaps possessed of choicer land, or better endowed with strength of body and mind, or blessed with many sons, stayed on. In their old age they could sit on the front porch and survey a vista of twenty or thirty or more acres open to the sunshine. Then their children took up the contest and conquered a few more acres...and so on, until the farms of yesteryear took shape.

They kept doing this until around 1880. That was the turning point. In 1871 Canada's first official census revealed that there were about three and one-quarter million acres under cultivation in the three Maritime provinces. In the next decade the acreage crept a little higher, peaked, and then went into a steady decline. Today it is only a third of what it was.

The same thing happened to many thriving villages. In 1881 Whycocomagh North in Cape Breton Island was a bustling community of 1,787. Besides rivalling Sydney in size, it was largely self-sufficient. As Charles W. Dunn recounts in his book *Highland Settler*, it had merchants, school teachers, inn-keepers, a shipwright, carriage-maker, wheelwright, tanner, two blacksmiths, and two tailors.

One could get anything from a ship to an education without leaving home.

Then the population drain began. By the time of the 1941 census Whycocomagh North had 696 persons left. Meanwhile Sydney had burgeoned to 28,305. The same tale could be repeated for hundreds of rural Maritime communities.

Where did all the people go? While Sydney and Halifax and Charlottetown and Saint John and Bathurst did absorb many of them, more often it was to 'the Boston States' and to Toronto that they emigrated. Many went Out West on the Harvest Excursion Train to seek work under wider skies. Some went on to British Columbia to work in the big woods. One doesn't travel far in New England or the West without meeting their offspring.

And why did they have to leave? How could they abandon their hard-won acres, their peaceful villages? To us, looking back with a certain nostalgia and perhaps naïveté, it seems strange.

Their reasons were many. Some, like the Acadians, were forced off at musket-point. Many were never cut out to be farmers. Some had no heirs to pass their land to. Others had sons but would not relinquish the reins in time to keep them home. Some had more children than the land could support. Many had poor land whose natural fertility was soon spent.

Ironically, the coming of the railroads helped. The first line from Truro in Nova Scotia to New Brunswick was opened in November 1872; the first train from Halifax arrived in Quebec City in July, 1876. Chuffing through the countryside, stitching together isolated hamlets whose inhabitants might not have gone to town more than once or twice a year hitherto, trains opened new vistas. And with the trains came the ubiquitous salesmen, pushing everything from apple peelers to mechanical reapers, from miracle cures to Parisian fashions. The trickle of store-bought goods released in 1844 by Eaton's first mail-order catalogue became a flood.

Rural life would never be the same again. On the surface it grew simpler. Relieved of the burden of so much self-reliance, one might have expected people to strike deeper roots where they were. The effect was otherwise.

Our carriage-maker in Whycocomagh soon found himself losing business to the Concord Stage Coach Company of New Hampshire. Our two blacksmiths were dismayed to learn that their customers were importing sundry ironwares from Montreal. Our tailors, though marvels with a needle, could not compete with rank on rank of Eaton's seamstresses stitching on eight-hour shifts in Toronto. Our shipwright was forced to hang up his tools as steam-powered iron hulls drove wooden wind-ships from the seas.

The subsistence farmer whose stony acres had been enough to support his family found that he could not support a motor car too. His shrewder neighbour, observing that everywhere the small enterprise was failing, resolved to extend his acreage and to mechanize. He bought up the failed farms around him and acquired the mechanical reaper and other labour-savers from Montreal. Later, finding his horses overtaxed to haul this gear, he replaced them with a tractor from Ontario. It didn't bother him that the tractor was no good in the woodlot. He had little time for logging now anyway. Besides, he had switched from wood to coal for heating (as later he would switch to oil), and he had seen the advantages of wire fencing over wooden.

One day, in the midst of marvelling at how his machines let one man do the work of five, he discovered that two of his sons were leaving for Boston and that the third was enlisting to fight in the

Great War. When old age forced him to quit, he auctioned everything off and moved to Boston too.

Thus the exodus. Except for a slight reversal during the Hard Times of the thirties, when the Depression wafted a few pilgrims back to the land, the trend has continued until recently. Tumbledown farmsteads and weedy fields tell the tale.

But lately things have changed. Land is being cleared again. This time it is being done differently. Now machine deposes muscle, oil upstages sweat. And the poor land is being bypassed for the best. Today a farmer can clear more acres in one year than his forebears could in a lifetime. And governments will help him do it.

Meanwhile, the pioneers sleep near their failed farms.

A few years back I helped to lay one of that breed to rest. Moody McMichael had been born in Kent County in New Brunswick around the time the exodus began, but had stayed home to help work the farm his grandfather had cleared on the West Branch of the St. Nicholas River. When I first met him he was in his late seventies and had retired to live with his daughter. Though small in stature he still possessed great physical strength and stamina.

My most vivid recollections of Moody show him shovelling out a long lane of waist-high snow, or cleaving thick birch bolts into stovewood. Though he punctuated the key motions with a grunt, it was not from exertion. His movements displayed the utmost economy. His output was prodigious, leaving younger men behind. He still knew how to work.

After we lowered him into his native soil in the West Branch cemetery, I stood back and let my eyes roam the circuit of his fields. Everywhere, advancing under cover of alder and goldenrod like soldiers, the dark spruces were moving in to take back his land for the owls and the bears.

—1977

• Earth-Time: A Glacial Revery •

*I*n *my mind I am standing at the foot of the ice cliffs, leaning back and squinting against the rising sun to see where, a long spear- throw above my head, the glacier meets the sky in a ragged line. Ice fills the world above our valley, chilling everything unless the wind is from the south.*

This morning there is no wind. The air smells dank. I shiver as it seeps through even my caribou cloak and leggings. To keep warm I resume picking my way over the rubble of boulders and fallen ice blocks that lie in rough heaps along the base of the ice wall.

As the sun warms the upper cliffs, huge chunks of ice come loose and cartwheel down the slope to my left, exploding upward as they hit the rocks. But this morning they seem to fall and burst in silence, so great is the din of running water. It is the earliest spring in memory. I move out to a safer distance.

From here I can see the water spilling down the glacier's face, snaking to and fro in smooth green gullies, spouting out of blue cracks, cascading off ledges in rainbows of colour. At my feet it gushes out from under the gravel and dirty ice, percolating among the stones, merging in streamlets that come together in brooks which join farther down the valley to become the Great River by whose banks I and my family and my uncles and aunts have lived all our lives, hunting and fishing and gathering. Jumping now from rock to slippery rock to cross a stream, I am glad I remembered to lard my skin leggings well with seal fat this morning.

The whoosh of a passing car jerks me out of my Pleistocene revery to find myself standing in a gravel pit behind a country church in Nova Scotia. I had spotted the pit while driving and had swung off the hot highway to get a breath of fresh air and to untangle my nerves. I had also hoped to learn something of the local geology.

Now my neck feels stiff from craning up to see where front-end loaders have laid open the spruce ridge for road gravel. Crumbling layers of pebbles and sand clearly label this as a place of glacial outwash. One hundred centuries ago the stones up there had formed the bed of a river fed by the millennia-long melting of the southern edge of the retreating Labrador Ice Sheet. That sheet had lain on our land for ten times as long, burying the place where I now stood under thousands of feet of groaning ice, ice whose slow-motion ebb and flow had built this rumpled landscape.

Down the valley to my right the floodplain shimmers like a mackerel in the sun, green in its winding streams. Across the whole valley are fans and bars and crescents of sand and gravel, which are covered and uncovered as the currents shift. The streams are milky with fertile rock dust from the glacier's endless grinding. Later, in the heat of our short summer, they will carry loads of sand and pebbles quietly rattling in the night. During storms even boulders are rolled along.

Less than two moons ago this water world was still locked in snow and ice. Then the north wind would swoop down off the icefields, moaning among our snow huts, driving the game into cover for weeks on end. Often it raised storms of fine dust that stung our eyes and raised knee-deep drifts of loess even on the glacier, drifts that lingered all summer to collect stray seeds and to sprout green plants that made soil and attracted wildlife and preserved the ice beneath it from melting—for a time.

But only for a time. For the glaciers are retreating. Even I in my short life time can sense a softening. My father sees it clearly. And my grandfather is sure of it. The great snows have failed. Winters come later and springs come sooner. The caribou and mastodon and bison summer farther north than ever before.

Even now, far out on the southern skyline, barely moving as they graze northward, I spot the first string of returning caribou. Still in their winter coats, they are all the colour of driftwood. Around and over them as they crop the lush grasses and first buttercups, cloud shadows slide like immense blue birds. It is a good day to be alive.

My neck feels stiff, but I feel refreshed; I have had a brush with geologic time, earth-time. The experience, like a walk under the stars, has cleared my mind of petty cares and restored my perspective. Yet I can take this medicine only in small doses. If I dwell on it, the whole idea of ice ages becomes preposterous; it is more fantastic than UFOs, more incredible than gods from outer space. To think that every so often the earth undergoes a natural refrigeration so that whole continents become white whistling wildernesses like today's

Antarctica or Greenland, and then to think that the earth defrosts itself and returns to smiling weather—it is almost too much. The mind flicks to another channel.

Yet it did happen. It happened at least seven times in the last few million years alone, they say. The proof lies all about us. The very landscapes outside our windows recall those stupendous events. Naturally we prefer to forget such things. We are like the kid I had on a nature hike once who, when asked how a huge boulder came to be perched atop a remote hill, replied, "Bulldozer."

To me that's a bit like finding a Sasquatch track by our doorstep and not bothering to investigate. Just for curiosity's sake the Ice Ages are worth looking into. Never mind that some experts now predict their return in a few centuries or even less. Probing for clues of the last visitation can be exciting enough, especially when it touches our daily lives so intimately.

❄ ITEM: You buy a new house and start to put in a lawn or garden, only to discover more rocks than you thought possible in one small patch of land. The more you rake them out the more they keep popping to the surface. Load after load you cart away, until you despair of ever coming to the end. But don't worry. You're in good company. The Swedes have the same problem. All northern peoples suffer from too many rocks. Glaciers are very untidy that way. Whatever is too hard to grind into powder they leave scattered over the countryside. (If you lived in Texas you wouldn't have that problem. The last few glaciations never reached south of Kansas, and the mess from the earlier ones has all weathered away.) Be thankful you don't have a ten-acre field to tidy up. The pioneers knew all about that. To come across one of their rockpiles or stone fences is a lesson in itself.

❄ ITEM: In parts of Nova Scotia's Lunenburg and Queens Counties, nearly every farm sits on the crown of a beautifully curved hill that rises broad and steep at one end and tapers like a whale's back to the other. Moreover, these whaleback hills or drumlins—each forty to a hundred feet high and as much as three-fourths of a mile long—are arranged in parallel clusters like a school of fish all swimming the same way. They were formed about ten miles back from the ice front, in districts underlaid with slate. Slate, when ground in water, makes clay. Clay is slippery, and under the moving ice— thinner and less heavy here than up-country in New

Brunswick or Labrador, where it was up to two miles thick—it gave just enough lubrication to let the sheet ride up and over its own debris. In the process it sculpted these lovely hills, leaving them with their tails all pointing the way the ice travelled. Halifax's Citadel Hill is itself a drumlin.

❊ ITEM: Out hiking, you come across a hilltop with bedrock as smooth as pavement. Surprised, you look closer and discover that the surface is scored with ancient scratches so straight they might have been drawn with a ruler. And they are all parallel. You ask around and learn that they were cut by fragments of quartz or some other hard rock frozen into the underside of the moving ice. Borne along under unimaginable weight, they scored the softer bedrock as a diamond scores glass.

❊ ITEM: A hundred miles off Nova Scotia lies foggy Sable Island, the only scrap of land in a lonely waste of ocean. How did it get here, this sandbar in the middle of nowhere? A glance at an undersea chart of the area offers a clue. Sable marks the edge of the continental shelf. During the 95,000 years of the last (or Wisconsin) glaciation, when the ice had drunk up so much sea that the Atlantic was nearly four hundred feet lower than it is today, most of the shelf off Eastern Canada was dry land. Over this shelf the ice sheet crept eastward, dumping billions of tons of rock and soil scoured from our uplands— enriching the sea bed by impoverishing the land. Most of the dumping occurred near the edge of the shelf, where the sheet met deep water and floated and broke up. As the ice waned and the sea reclaimed its territory, only the highest of those mounds stayed above water. For a time there must have been many Sables. Even now, say Banks fishermen, there are shallow places where the sea breaks into surf in heavy weather. But Sable Island is the only dry land left. Its nearest counterparts are Cape Cod and Manhattan Island. And because the polar caps are still melting, the sea is still rising.

Ten thousand years is only a tick on the geologic clock. But to our workaday minds it can seem utterly remote and unreal. For me, glacial phenomena like Sable Island and bedrock scratches and whaleback hills and rocks in the garden help bring it home.

I think the place where I feel most keenly the reality of the last Ice Age is on the open tundralike boglands of eastern Newfoundland

in spring. It is a prairie world of ochre and russet, wine and gray, broken by scattered granite ridges like pods of breaching whales. Little ponds, tea-coloured in repose, flash suddenly silver as stray gusts fret their surfaces. Wind is a constant presence. Ancient spruce and fir hug the earth in dense mats to escape its rude elbowing.

As I walk over one such mat a willow ptarmigan rockets from cover, sets its white-patched wings and sails downwind to safety. And from upwind comes the scolding cry of a yellowlegs scared from its nest. At my feet are recent signs of caribou.

Though it is June, drift ice still clogs the bay. Swiftly a gray bank of fog rolls in, chilling the air with the breath of Polar regions, muffling the rote of the sea. Through the mist, upended boulders loom as large as cottages. Everything is sodden. Everything looks scraped to the bone. Everything exhales an air of nameless dread, as if one had stumbled on the lair of hostile giants. Here it is easier to believe that an Ice Age really did happen.

And, yes, could happen again.

—*1978*

• A Simple Handslide •

Whenn the Arabs started turning the energy screws on us a few
years back, I went out and bought a small woodlot and a
wood stove and commenced cutting my own firewood. I knew full
well I wouldn't save much on the deal by the time I'd bought a power
saw and likely a tractor; I was also well aware that getting one's own
fuelwood means a lot of hard work.

It was more a matter of pride: our grandfathers had done without Mid-East oil; why couldn't we?

While in this rebellious frame of mind I resolved to go a step
further and build myself a handslide, one like the old-timers used
for hauling out their winter's wood when they couldn't afford a
horse. Yes, and I might as well go back to the pulp saw and axe while
I was at it.

In the process I learned a few things about handslides, about
old-timers, about myself.

The first lesson was that I didn't know how to build the thing.
Oh, I could picture it well enough: a small wooden sled eight or so
feet long, loaded with birch or spruce sticks, pulled by a bewhiskered
old fellow smoking a pipe as he plodded home through the snowy
woods, a rope over his shoulder, the shaft under his arm. Yes. But
when it came to actual construction, I couldn't remember.

So I wrote my father. Surely he would know. A week later he
replied, enclosing a sketch. "I'm no artist," he wrote, "but this should
give you the general idea." A few days later he sent another sketch
with some details he'd overlooked, adding this postscript: "Be sure
to lay out your trail on the level—downhill if possible. Building the
sled should be easy. It's after that the *real* work begins."

As it turned out, even building the sled wasn't all that easy. The winter was to be almost over before I finally took it to the woods.

My first problem was the curved runners. The other wooden parts could be bought at a lumber yard; runners must be handmade. Right off, I saw that even a simple handslide takes some planning. You can't just up and make one. In fact a handslide, like a boat, starts with choosing a crooked tree in the woods a year before. By rights the log from which my runners would be sawn should have been drying over the rafters in the barn all summer. If I went out now and cut one and used it green, the runners would warp out of line in no time.

A friend came to my rescue. "I've got the clear thing for you," he said, "—a piece of birch someone stored in my barn years ago and forgot. Just rip it down the middle and you're in business." Delighted, I thanked him and took it home.

But when I set about sawing it I found the going much slower than I'd bargained for. Birch is a pretty hard wood. Worse, my handsaw needed sharpening. (I'd often intended to learn how.) Cutting with the grain is slow going, even with soft woods. After ten minutes I'd made almost no progress. The old-timers would have done it by hand, I knew. Oh well, I said, there are only so many hours in a day—and went and got the thing sawed by another friend. He has an electric bench saw.

Next I needed metal shoes for the runners. A century ago this would have been a job for the local blacksmith. Our nearest smithy had closed ten years before. Luckily we still had a couple of those old-fashioned hardware stores of the kind where nails are sold loose, where the floorboards creak and there are cobwebby places forgotten even by the management.

"Oh yes, sir," smiled the dapper young clerk. "We have the material you speak of in various widths and thicknesses, what size do you need?" And he led me to a cavernous basement lit by dusty bare bulbs hung from great hand-hewn beams. While we were inspecting the piles of steel strips an older clerk happened by and asked what we wanted. When I explained, he shook his head. "This here stuff ain't what you need," he said.

"It isn't?" said Dapper and I.

Older Clerk shook his head. "No run to it," he said gravely. When I asked what that meant he pointed out that soft steel like the stuff at our feet tended to scratch easily and stick to the snow. He advised me to try the local foundry for special shoe steel, a much harder type.

The foundry people assured me they could indeed sell me what I wanted. However, since I needed so little, would I mind waiting a few weeks until a shipment came in, at which time they would certainly notify me?

Months passed with no word. After many phone calls I finally gave it up for a bad job and went back to the hardware store and bought the stuff with no run to it.

Now I was ready for actual construction.

Already it was mid-winter. Having neither barn nor workshop, I had to build it on the kitchen floor. Dad's instructions were simple to follow. A few evenings and it was finished.

"On the level...downhill if possible...," echoed my father's voice as I tramped the snowy woods one Saturday morning seeking the best route, the best compromise between directness and slope. Until then I'd never really noticed how many humps and hollows my woodlot had. Even the seemingly level ground was rumpled with cradle-hills. I began to appreciate the skill it takes to properly locate a road by eye.

The route selected, I marked it with axe blazes and cut any trees and brush that stood in the way. I noted with satisfaction, that, compared to a tractor, a handslide takes very little right-of-way. That afternoon I hitched the sled to the car and towed it to the woodlot three miles down the road. Hauling the empty sled from road to woodpile was a snap. My handiwork rode the snowy billows behind me like a gull on the waves. Obviously my idea of making the runners twice the recommended width was paying off. Still, the sled seemed a bit heavier than I'd expected.

At the woodpile I eagerly tossed on what seemed a reasonable load of maple and birch. Placing the rope over one shoulder and the rigid steering shaft under my arm (like the old fellow in my mental picture), I leaned into the load. I am fairly strong. Yet nothing budged. The sled might as well have been set in concrete. I put more into it. Still no go. Then I recalled how the sled dog, Buck, when he pulled that record load in *Call of the Wild*, had first jerked it from side to side. Of course. That must be part of the reason for the rigid shaft. Common sense.

Even common sense wouldn't move this load more than a few feet. I had simply piled on too much for the available horsepower. Glancing around to see if anyone was watching, I removed four or five of the smaller logs. Again I harnessed up and tried. Now I could pull it all right, but the first small uphill grade stopped me. Maybe, I panted, snow conditions were wrong today? Perhaps I should wait until the weather was either colder or milder?

At last, after several starts and stops and further jettisoning of cargo, I succeeded in moving one load to roadside. By the time I'd made several trips I was bushed. On subsequent weekends I was glad to enlist help with the hauling. Later we got a tractor. A sled just took too much time. I felt dispirited, unworthy of my ancestors. Not only were they tougher, they must have been smarter too.

I went to an older friend and told him my troubles. We got out the sketches. Right away it was apparent that my sled was built too heavy. Whereas the original was designed to be made entirely of spruce, mine had birch runners and Douglas-fir bunks—both much heavier woods. Worse, I had deliberately doubled the runner width, reasoning that this would give me greater buoyancy in deep snow. I'd failed to consider that this would also double the friction—and that, in any case, a handslide trail is supposed to be tramped smooth with snowshoes before any hauling is done. Buoyancy wasn't a factor. On top of this, I had staggered the bolts that held the runner shoes on, thereby adding still more drag. Finally, I wasn't really in shape to play the workhorse. Cross-country skiing is all very well, but it just doesn't compare with old-time hard work.

Looking at it all from this angle, I felt better. And I learned a new respect for the skill and ingenuity and patience and stamina of my 'uneducated' forebears.

Lately, in fact, I've been thinking of making another handslide —the right way this time. But what would I do with the first one? After all, with more power it would work fine. Doesn't look bad either. Weathered nice and gray. Someone might buy it for an antique. Hadn't my farmer neighbour already mistaken it for an old one his father once used? Or, someone might buy it for a lawn ornament. I've seen worse things on lawns....

Yes, I'll draft the ad right now:

FOR SALE

Sturdy wooden sled in authentic old-time design. Ideal for hauling firewood or supplies behind snowmobile, pony or Newfoundland dog. Also makes a unique lawn ornament and conversation piece. Only used once.

—1979

Winter Thoughts

There is a fraternity of the cold, to which I am glad
to belong.

E.B. White,
One Man's Meat

• Bonfire Night •

Ever notice how the youngsters go daft after supper in the fall? They're at it outside now, prancing about in the dusk with bed sheets flapping around their shoulders, whooping like fiends, cheeks flushed, breathing hard, eyes glazed with dread and delight.

What brings this on?

The easy answer is Hallowe'en. The witches and hobgoblins and jack-o'-lanterns have got them all worked up, we say. But this is too pat. I think Hallowe'en is just an effect, not the cause. I never laid eyes on a real jack-o-lantern till I was twenty, yet I can recall being overtaken by the self-same madness around the age of ten.

It was a subtle thing. It crept up on you. The first twinge came when you went out to play after supper some evening and saw how low the sun had suddenly got. The next one struck when you felt the first hint of frost. Other events that could trigger it were the reappearance of the Northern Lights, the sight of goldenrods gone silvery, the sound of geese honking somewhere up in the night sky, a skim of ice on morning puddles, supper by lamplight, apples on the ground...things like that. Common symptoms were a lump in the throat, a catch in the breath, tightness in the chest, a quickening of the pulse.

The cure? A bonfire!

Here again it is easy to mix cause and effect. The history books tell us that Bonfire Night, as practised until recently in parts of Britain and her Dominions every November 5 (and still practised in New-foundland—Torbay had a fine Bonfire celebration last year) is supposed to commemorate Guy Fawkes' unsuccessful attempt in 1605 to blow the English Parliament (and James I) sky-high. But, as any sensible person knows, nothing could be more natural and practical when the nights start to close in and the air turns unfriendly than to light a fire. In my opinion, the Gunpowder Plot merely supplied a convenient date: the rest was autumn madness.

Now for driving back the cold and dark your bonfire has it all over a candle in a pumpkin. "The bigger the better" was our motto. The only limit was our appetite for work. Already by late September, on the way to and from school, we were collecting burnable odds and ends. By early October the work had begun in earnest. Every fine Saturday we made for the woods with axes and saws. It was a regular woods operation. Parties of six or eight boys and an occasional girl attacked small spruce and fir, worried them to the ground, lugged them to the chosen spot and piled them for drying. Each party had its own pile off by itself, on a hill if possible. By the time we were done, the whole area was studded with those pointy, gnawed stumps that are the trademark of young axepersons and of beavers.

At last the great Night is come.

Stumbling uphill through the dark woods to the site, we shiver a little and not from cold alone. As we near the shaggy mountain of trees, boxes, boots, planks, hay and whatall, our hearts beat faster. There it stands, looming like a mammoth against Orion and his troop of winter stars. And here we stand, like a circle of dwarf Druids, awed into silence, waiting.

Someone steps forward, matchbox in hand. Stoops. One uncertain scrape, two scrapes, a few sparks...nothing. (Those *Seadog* matches always were kind of brittle.) Once more cold fingers fumble, this time managing a momentary spurt of fire that makes the woods seem darker than ever. We inch closer. Somebody swears, snatches the box, strikes three or four matches together, rams them flaming under the handful of birch bark. As the fire licks the pink shreds and curls around the red needles a sound like that of bacon frying is heard, followed by a sound like hail on dry grass, rising to a sound like car tires rolling on loose gravel.

"She's really goin' now!"

And, gulping air fiercely, the fire would claw its way up through the pile and burst forth as if bent on roasting us all. At the blast we'd fall back. With the clearing now as bright as day, we'd start to run and jump, our shadows swooping like huge black birds, our voices lost in the seething roar, our eyes mesmerized by coruscations of violet and crimson and gold.

For an hour or so that was how it was with us. A stranger to our ritual would have declared us berserk. We cavorted until we were exhausted, we shouted until we were hoarse. And whenever the blaze died down and the shadows began to steal back one of us would toss on a tree or two. Often we'd do this just to get a shower of sparks (which we, in our innocence, called *flankers*, a fine old English word now missing from most dictionaries). A good way to get dizzy was to try to track one flanker as it looped and dived among the others until it winked out.

When we had nothing more to throw on, when even energetic poking failed to produce any more pyrotechnics and the blaze was subsiding, we would draw close to bask in the heat and to peer into the lattice of charred trees, here light against light, here resembling an armada of galleons ablaze, there suggesting the face of beautiful lady, here conjuring up the Devil himself.

Later still we'd see who could jump the farthest over the glowing coals without melting their rubbers or singeing their socks. Or we'd flip glowing sticks end over end against the sky. Or spell out our names with them in the dark.

When nothing was left but a ruby glow we would bury bottles and jars to melt into curious shapes overnight. One year we burnt the ends out of empty evaporated milk cans and make a dandy pipe for a homemade tin stove. A few of us seized the opportunity to smoke cigarettes made of brown wrapping paper stuffed with dried alder leaves. The more genteel toasted slices of bread over the coals.

Meanwhile, on nearby hills similar ceremonies ran their courses. One by one the yellow beacons would flare, flicker and die. Sometimes rain would speed the process.

At last it was time to trudge home. Again the cold and dark enveloped us. But now we didn't mind. Now winter could come as soon as it liked. For all we cared, the sun could fall out of the sky before supper and not rise again till noon. We had exorcised our subconscious dread. And all it had cost was a few little trees that nobody would miss, some holes in our socks and sweaters which patient mothers would darn with appropriate grumbling, the odd burnt boot, a faint opprobrium of woodsmoke about our persons until the next wash.

They say there's a little arson in each of us. We're reminded of this whenever the pyromaniac starts a forest fire or burns a barn, or when we catch ourselves hankering to chase a fire truck. Even so, the bonfire—at least in my experience—was just the opposite. Stripped of its political-religious connotations it was simply Light versus Dark, Warmth versus Cold—even, if you will, Life versus Death—all rolled up in a child's autumn rite.

These days, a bonfire on the front lawn would only bring the fire department. All the more reason, then, to let the youngsters race and shriek and go off their rockers once a year. If grownups did it there'd be talk; but the kids have got the right idea. Winter will be plenty long enough.

—1978

• The Winter House •

I can see our winter house now, its warm bulk muffled in the snowbanks of my childhood. I can see the golden gleam of its small windows against the February dusk. I can see the dark wall of spruce rising behind it to the cold stars, and trace the vagaries of spark showers from the stove pipe whenever a junk turns in the fire.

Standing outside our winter house in memory, I can hear things, too. My mother is drawing water from the barrel in the porch: 'plash' goes the dipper; 'thunk' the lid. Then the table resumes its rhythmic squeak as she returns to kneading bread. The droning voice is the Gerald S. Doyle radio bulletin, recounting tonight's war news. The raucous snore-and-wheeze is my grandfather enjoying his rocking chair.

We called it a Winter House because it was where we lived in winter, to keep warm. Our real house, the Summer House, was too chilly for winter habitation. It had sawdust under the clapboards everywhere, but still the wind sighed in here and there, circumventing the mats and blankets which my father stuffed under doors and along sills on bitter nights. One summer he fetched stout logs, did a lot of chopping and chinking, and built the Winter House. That fall we moved in. The happiest winters of my childhood followed.

Some would have called it a log cabin, I suppose. On the outside it was. But inside was a home, and a spacious one, too. We had a big kitchen-living room, three bedrooms, a pantry and a porch. The doors inside made never a sound, for they were of smoky cotton. Green sheathing paper cozied the walls and echoed summer. An *Ideal* cookstove cheered the nights. Lamplight mellowed all.

"Tea time!" My mother's treble call, finding us playing somewhere in the snowscape at dusk, meant the real end of day; a vespers bell ringing me home after sunset, night by night. In the porch the sweeping ritual proceeded, and the day's snow flew like water when a wet dog shakes himself. But the caked snow was often too tenacious for broom or brush, and had to be plucked like feathers from a chicken, until the mat would be dotted with these wool-whiskered knobs.

Supper was by lamplight in our Winter House, for the days were already short when we left the Summer House each November. There is magic in an old lamp. Ours was handsome whether lighted or not; but when set in its bracket over the table, with its lambent flame seized and amplified by the silvered reflector and beamed about the room, it seemed that no chandelier could surpass it. My mother polished the fluted chimney each morning with a page from *The Family Herald* or *The Toronto Weekly Star*. The sound she made was like frosty snow underfoot. She would fill the bowl with kerosene, snip-snip the wick into shape, and set the lamp on high again.

I smile to recall the potato she kept over the oil-can spout.

Moose, caribou and rabbit were our fresh meat in winter, isolated as we were when the river froze; so these often steamed on the supper plates, along with potatoes, turnips, carrots or cabbage from the cellar. Salt beef was the standby—and still seems to me the only proper flavouring for potatoes. (I have friends who differ with me on this point, but I once converted a Danish forester to cooking salt beef with his vegetables.)

To wake to the smell and sound of caribou steaks frying in pork fat and onions on a winter morning beats bacon and eggs and coffee all to bits, especially when you are nine years old. It's a good breakfast to go to school and learn arithmetic on. It seems disloyal to say so, but we always fancied that Dad could fry wild meat better than Mom. He thought so too.

Perhaps it was natural that he should be able to, since in those days he was a trapper. Every month he made the round of his traplines, and one of my most colourful mental images is that of my father readying sled and dogs for that trek. For a week before, Mom would roll out bread and buns, and then there would be enough. At last, when everything was aboard and lashed fast—traps, axe, kettle, and pot; bread, butter, and beans; tea, sugar, molasses and fat pork; snowshoes and the rest—then the eager dogs would be slipped into their harnesses. A melee of yelps by the porch door, a crunch of ice and squeak of frozen wood, and he would be off. We would wave, then turn and go to school. Mom would wave, then turn and be father and mother for a few weeks.

The homecomings were just as memorable. Usually they were after dark, but as soon as we heard panting dogs, we knew who it was. Before the sleigh was halted we would burst out, and for me the special memory is one of smell and touch: fir boughs and wood-smoke and scrubbing-brush whiskers; and afterward, a pocketful of spruce gum would be mine.

Christmases in the Winter House were the best of any. I still believed in a red-jacketed Santa Claus then. One December, only a few nights before Christmas Eve, I was not behaving very well. I was advised that Saint Nick gave no gifts to naughty boys such as I, and that at that selfsame moment he might be flying by on his reindeer, making his last-minute check on good boys and bad.

I grew still. Suddenly our snow-blanketed roof came alive with the trampling of little hooves—and my parents heard them too! I raced to bed and burrowed deep.

And the hoof-prints were there the next morning—partly snowed out, but unmistakable; everywhere dimpling the low roof. But over at the northwest corner was a curious thing: two sets of tracks led off on to a high snowbank, meandered to the level snow, and ended at the barn. Now, we kept goats... and it was not hard for me to deduce how the two frisky animals, escaping their pen in the night, took advantage of the low eaves and high, hard-packed snowdrift to try their climbing skill.

Believing it was the hard part.

That was the Christmas I got the red sleigh. Or rather, it was the Christmas I learned I was to get one soon. In reply to my scrawly note, Santa left a scrawly one of his own:

> Dear Gary:
> Your red sleigh will come on the
> steamer next week.
>
> Love,
> Santa Claus

I was bursting with pride, I remember. He, Santa Claus, *had written that note with my pencil, and on paper out of my scribbler.* I knew this, because I had heard him rummaging in my book-bag, which was hung on the post of my bunk, very early on Christmas morning—and had discovered that the page missing in my yellow scribbler and the page with the note were *one and the same*.

Another cause for pride was that this wonderful Father Christmas always took time to enjoy a glass of milk and slab of chocolate cake at our table, year by year. It was some time before I noted the connection between this and my father's fondness for the same snack.

One week and one day afterward, when there was ice forming in the Bay, the steamer arrived on her last trip for the season with freight for my grandfather's general store. Atop the jumble of bed springs and onion sacks in the scow as it neared the wharf was something scarlet and gold that glinted in the sunlight. When it got close enough I could read the magic inscription: *Rocket Racer*. The battered sled my father had made lay unused and dusty in the woodshed thereafter.

One winter it snowed a great deal. It snowed till every fence was erased from the landscape, and did not cease until every tree and house seemed half-submerged in a white flood. The Christmas our goats climbed on to the roof was green compared to it. Or so it seems. When the sky got blue again our Winter House was eaves-deep in the whiteness.

Men had to come and dig us out—although I would have let things remain as they were. At breakfast there came a scratching at the snow-crusted pane: someone's mittened hand was clearing a path for the daylight. At the same time we heard a scraping and grunting outside the porch: that was my portly grandfather shovelling into the great breakers of snow that walled us in. We could picture him and we smiled in spite of our plight. For my Grandpa shovelled snow in a manner all his own. Straight over his left shoulder would fly each charge, accompanied by a grunt. It was dangerous to stand behind him when he shovelled snow.

That spring we were flooded out. We were on low ground, so when all the snow melted and Clarke's Brook behind the meadow overtopped its banks, it was only a few nights before the water stole under our door. I woke to the sound of splashing, and was carried in high glee from my bunk. At daylight that March morning we beat a retreat to the Summer House, preferring drafts to drowning. I didn't go back that year, except to enjoy the odd sensation of skating in my bedroom.

And that was life for a little boy in a Winter House. Many of my playmates lived the same way. Not all summer houses were as drafty as ours, of course; custom seems to have played some part in this hibernal pattern of living. Certainly economy didn't, for the only actual saving was in fuel-wood—which was abundant, anyway. Poverty explained the pattern with some, for they lived in their log houses winter and summer. But a Winter House is no good for summer living. Their children missed some poignant memories.

No, it was not poverty. Rather, it was a peculiar affluence which our forebears bequeathed us when they abandoned their sea-pounded fishing hamlets for sheltered, wooded inlets like our bay. Their comrades who stayed to ply oar and jigger pinned on them the derisive label of 'Baymen'. But the plenitude of fresh meat, garden space and wood soon salved the sting away. Soon, in fact, as they sat in their snug cabins and chatted of harder times, they came to adopt 'Outsiders' as the name for their seafaring brethren, and 'the Outside' as the place where they lived.

Thus the Winter House occupied a transition zone between that century and this. Sitting now within earshot of passing cars in this modern house, I feel gratitude that my generation was able to inherit, while yet children, some of that pioneering tradition.

I can see it now—a Christmas-card cottage come to life; snow-mantled, tree-fenced, bright-windowed, in a lilac dusk.

—*1961*

• In Praise of Wood Stoves •

The first wood stove I ever owned I cut from a juice tin with my mother's best scissors when I was eight. It would have worked, too. I installed it behind the hen house, stuffed it with birch bark and wood chips from the woodpile, poked my stolen match in at the air-hole, and settled down to admire the quick yellow flame licking the pink shreds of bark and fingering the slivers of wood. But just as the tin began to turn nice shades of blue and gold, my mother's shadow fell across the proceedings. I and my stove went separate ways, never to meet again. But the hen house was saved.

Playing with fire was more natural for youngsters then. We saw that big people did it all the time. Morning after morning we woke to the sounds of fathers and mothers lighting the fire. And in the winter we would hug the quilts until the last possible moment before making that desperate dash, clothes under arm, for the warm kitchen. In those days you could nearly always see your breath in the bedroom on a winter morning, not to mention ice in the chamber pot.

So I early developed a fascination with wood stoves. And somewhere, in that secret part of a child's mind where dreams are stored, I must have resolved to possess one for myself some day.

Now I own three.

But it took a few crises to bring this about. As long ago as 1970, in fact, my wife and I had admired a fine old stove displayed at a fall fair. It was the *Queen Cook*, then made by the Enterprise Foundry in Sackville, N.B. We brought home a brochure and pinned it up, imagining the cozy glow and the nickel Queen Victoria medallions gleaming on the oven doors. But our interest was mostly in form rather than function, and the idea was never consummated.

Then came the oil crisis. And after that, several windstorms which knocked out our power for hours and even days at a time. We began to realize that the old energy security was gone.

Huddling in one room and cooking over the fireplace was all right for an occasional lark. But this looked more serious. One had only to read the papers to realize that the days of easy energy were slipping away. I resolved to find a good stove that would provide both warmth and hot food when things went wrong. Reasoning that ranges cook well but make slow and indifferent heaters, while box stoves heat well but will hardly boil a kettle, I looked for a compromise.

The *Queen Cook* came to mind. But alas, by this time Enterprise had temporarily stopped making it.

Then, three winters ago, in a woods camp in western Nova Scotia, I came across its twin: the *Perfect Cook* made by Lunenburg Foundry and Engineering in Lunenburg. Stoves like this were a standby in small logging camps before roads and motor vehicles did away with isolation. Watching it heat that drafty camp and cook our meals, I knew this stove with its spray of oak leaves on the oven was

for me. (Besides, I find oak leaves more congenial than Queen Victoria's graven scowl.)

So I ordered one. I had to wait two years; the sudden demise of a master fitter put the *Perfect* out of production until a new fitter could be found and trained. Meanwhile I tried out an old *Queen Cook*, and an even older box stove.

Now we wouldn't want to be without a wood stove again. With a few cords of mostly home-cut wood I've halved our heating bill. Now winter gales and power failures hold fewer terrors for us. The oil is still there when we need it, but we depend on it less. It's a good feeling.

But the best part of owning these stoves has been the learning.

For one thing, they taught us why the old-time kitchen was the natural center of the home. It wasn't the couch or the rocking chair that did it; it was the physical center of warmth in an otherwise cool house. Dogs and cats and people alike were drawn to it like filings to a magnet.

Modern homes lack this focus. Minor adjustments can be made to registers and thermostats, but most parts still get equal heat. In other words, central *heating* affords no central *warmth*, no place to dry wet mittens or toast cold toes. For the sake of one or two rooms the whole house is kept more or less warm.

A good stove also radiates a kind of psychological warmth. As soon as we set up the *Perfect*, even though it was in the same room with the television, there was no doubt that it could hold its own with the *Six Million Dollar Man*. For a time, anyway.

Another thing our stoves taught us was the lore of firewood-making. Our forebears understood very well that wood is not mere wood, nor a tree merely a tree. Just as there is sirloin and sausage, so there are good woods and poor woods. Any pioneer who couldn't tell poplar from apple was in for a cold winter and soggy bread. Fortunately, most of the settlers came over with a fair knowledge of the art, since wood was the main fuel in the Old World of that day. They even had jingles to help them remember... like this string of couplets from England:

> Beech wood fires are bright and clear
> > If the logs are kept a year.
> Birch and fir logs burn too fast,
> > Blaze up bright and do not last.
> Elm wood burns like a churchyard mould;
> > E'en the very flames are cold.

Poplar gives a bitter smoke,
  Fills your eyes and makes you choke.
Apple wood will scent your room
  With an incense like perfume.
Oak and maple, if dry and old,
  Keep away the winter cold.
But ash wood wet and ash wood dry,
  A King shall warm his slippers by.

                                      Anon.

Ash is not that plentiful in our corner of Canada—and what there is would be better used in Indian baskets and canoe paddles. But Maritimers enjoy ample stocks of hard and soft maple, beech and oak. Newfoundland has birch and larch and good black spruce, with fir as a filler. Even those who own no woodland can usually lease short-term fuelwood cutting rights from the provincial forest services, most of whom are anxious to have this under-utilized forest resource put to better use. And even if one lacks a power chain saw (as I do), a pulp saw and axe will do the job if speed isn't critical.

It's hard to describe the satisfaction that comes from cutting one's own firewood and piling it rank on rank in the woodshed against the coming cold. It's not just the fresh air and exercise. Felling each tree, you muse on how it will heat your kitchen or family room a few months hence—for it should have time to dry. Stacking the pieces, you ponder the beauty of their varied textures, from birch rind as immaculate as fresh bond paper to maple bark as rough as rock. And as you bask in the warmth on the first wintry night, you can reflect that even though your work has left a messy hole in the forest, its emptiness is not like the emptiness of an abandoned coal mine or a sucked-dry oil well.

For the forest is self-renewing. This space will refill itself. Only a year or two hence there will be scores of vigorous shoots ringing your stumps. Moreover, if you should return in winter and study the new shoots you will see the signs of wildlife enjoying the banquet you have set: neat slanting cuts where snowshoe hare have nibbled, and frazzled ends where whitetail deer or moose have browsed. Years later, when the hardwood brush has outgrown the reach of hare or deer, you may spot a ruffed grouse clipping aspen and birch buds for supper. The patchwork cuttings of bygone days were good for forest and wildlife alike. You can't say the same for coal pits or oil wells.

Of course, there's some fire hazard with wood stoves. But oil furnaces have been known to blow up. Stuck down in the basement and seldom seen except by the service man, furnaces tend to be forgotten until they act up. Gas and electric stoves have been known to catch fire too. A wood stove on the other hand is in plain sight and gets constant attention. At least it should. It if does, and if pipes and chimneys are kept clean and in good repair, and the whole thing properly set up, a good stove is safer than most fireplaces.

Unfortunately, most insurance companies still don't see it that way. Educating them will take time. North America's current boom in stove sales should help—provided stove-makers maintain high standards. Meanwhile, people are unlikely to stop buying and insuring at high rates a far more dangerous device—the family motor car.

Another lesson we learned is that society is overheated. I soon found that by filling the box stove with good hardwood at bedtime, we didn't need the furnace at night except in the severest weather, when the pipes might have frozen. One small stove kept the chill off. And this was just an old stove, with none of the modern features like airtight fittings, special baffles, and primary and secondary draft control to eke the last calorie from each stick of wood.

We just don't need all that warmth at night—or even by day. Turning up the thermostat in the daytime is doubtless easier than donning a sweater; but isn't it a bit like washing the car when water is rationed? As for leaving it up at night when a few extra blankets could keep us snug, that's worse—and unhealthy to boot. With today's houses it's unlikely we'll freeze in our beds. At 68°F we're more likely to die of clogged sinuses or the common cold.

There is one hazard though. Baldheads like me have to watch it. About four o'clock in the morning on coldish nights the old dome gets chilly. This has taught me one more thing: the value of a night-cap. Lately I've been hinting for somebody to make me one. But I'm getting nowhere. They don't understand.

They figure I want a drink.

—1978

• Ice Age •

Perhaps it was the cool, wet June we had this year. Three times I seeded corn and three times the results were spotty. Or perhaps it was the book on glaciation that I was reading at the time. And it might have been my lifelong love of the spare landscape of the North. But this summer I began to imagine that, yes, a new Ice Age might come, that everything we take for granted—dependable weather, the punctual march of seasons, even the shape of the land itself—are not permanent fixtures. And this led me further to muse on what consternation and dismay and havoc another visitation of ice would wreak, and what, if any, good might come of it.

The first thing to grasp is the slowness of the process. Centuries might elapse before anyone was certain a new Ice Age was even on the way, and millennia more before the thing was in full bloom. So mentally I speeded the movie up. And for a starting point I picked something we saw in Newfoundland on vacation last July. Or perhaps it picked me.

It was early morning, and we had just spilled off the ferry *Marine Nautica* at Port aux Basques with scores of other motor vehicles, and were beetling inland through the coastal hills, making time before the day fulfilled its promise of being a scorcher. Being geologically-minded, I couldn't help but note the abundant evidence of glaciation all around us; but I was somehow unprepared for the spectacle, when we broke onto the open heathland a few miles later, of snow on the flanks of the Long Range Mountains dead ahead. It often happens after a heavy winter that snow will linger all summer in sheltered hollows high on the Long Range. But these patches seemed larger than normal. And I fancied they looked menacing, as if they had no intention of leaving this summer, or next, or for several thousand to come. Which really set me thinking. What if...?

What if next year the tourists in Cape Breton looked up in August to see such snowfields glimmering on the slopes of the Craignish Hills above Whycocomagh?

What if in the same month airline pilots traversing New Brunswick's highlands looked down from 25,000 feet to see Mount Carleton mantled in snow? And suppose that each succeeding summer those winter accumulations expanded, eventually meeting and coalescing with other snow fields until throughout Atlantic Canada the uplands were decidedly Arctic in appearance throughout the year and there was no doubt Something Was Wrong?

For that is how it would happen. First the cooler high ground would collect snow and retain it, just as it does now the world over at high altitudes and high latitudes. The top of Mount Kilimanjaro in equatorial Africa is always robed in white, and in the Swiss Alps the glaciers are always within a few miles of certain high-altitude villages. Indeed, the villagers monitor these slow-moving rivers of ice with care, knowing that as recently as the seventeenth century several hamlets—like Chamonix south of Lake Geneva—were overwhelmed by them and that the glaciers played such havoc for three hundred years.

All it took to trigger the process then was a drop of a few degrees Fahrenheit in the mean annual air temperature. Exactly what causes such cooling—dust clouds from volcanic activity, changes in solar radiation, mountain building—was and is unknown. All we know for sure is that, in the last two million years, parts of North America and Europe were buried under mile-thick ice sheets several times, with intervening warm spells much like the one we live in. And that the peak of the last inundation was some 15,000 to 20,000 years ago, followed by a smaller influx 2,500 to 3,000 years ago, and then by the mini-Ice Age mentioned above.

Scary, isn't it?

But no scarier than the assorted nuclear and other man-made horrors disturbing our sleep these days. In fact, the onset of a new Ice Age might even do some good, at least in the beginning. For there is a good chance that the super-powers, once they knew for sure we were in for it, would turn their attention from the mathematics of the Strategic Defence Initiative and Mutual Assured Destruction to the even more stupendous feats of engineering needed to assure survival in a global ice-box. The new threat would create a strong demand for Canadian and Finnish expertise in northern living, and the older Inuit and Lapp would suddenly find themselves the gurus of an old technology. Atlantic Canadians would have to give up their cherished pastime of Ottawa-bashing and settle down to becoming truly self-sufficient—because pretty soon most of Canada would be worse off than we. Northern nations would be the first to feel the pinch. Wild swings in the weather, along with persistently cool summers and mild snowy winters, would be among the first symptoms, say the experts. No Big Freeze—although cold snaps are part of it. Just plenty of snow each winter, and too little heat to get rid of it all each summer. A drop of 5°C in mean annual air temperature is enough to do it.

Gardeners would be among the first to note the change. Our tomatoes and squash would tell us. Maritime dairy farmers now locked into corn silage would grow tired of harvesting knee-high cattle corn and go back to traditional hay. Fruit growers would lose more and more of their crops to early and late frosts. Potatoes would become a doubtful proposition. People forget that in 1816, "The Year Without a Summer"—an event much less well known than the 1845-48 Irish potato famine with its horrendous death toll—Ireland lost 737,000 to famine. The massive 1815 explosion of Indonesia's Tambora volcano, which threw a veil of dust into the stratosphere that lowered temperatures worldwide, very likely helped cause it.

As the upland snow cover deepened and spread, lowland weather would worsen. Rain, drizzle and fog mixed with cool dry spells would be standard summer fare. Radio announcers who imagine their chief end in life is to glorify sunshine and enjoy it forever would pack their bags for warmer climes—good riddance. Icebergs—common off southern California during the last Ice Age—would grow so plentiful that the oil rigs would have to come ashore for good. The Newfoundland and Prince Edward Island ferries would soon be icebound in port, followed by the Digby and Yarmouth boats. Increasingly, stray polar bears would turn up in Cape Breton and farther south. (One turned up in Gander a few years ago.)

The fishery would be a disaster. Faced with massive snow-removal costs, town, highway and railroad administrators would clamour for subsidies, and services would break down. Snow tires would be legal year-round. Airlines would do a booming business taking people on one-way trips south—when weather permitted. Energy costs would soar, and there would be fears that

Beechwood and Wreck Cove and Churchill Falls would freeze up. Sales of kerosene heaters and wood stoves would soar. The forests would take a beating—but the spruce budworm problem would disappear.

When the upland snow sheet was thick enough for the upper layers to start turning into the rounded crystals called *firn*, and the *firn* into the true, foliated glacier-ice that flows like cold molasses only slower, then certain high areas like Mount Carleton, Labrador's Torngat Mountains, and Newfoundland's Lewis Hills, Nova Scotia's Cape Breton Highlands and perhaps even its thousand-foot Cobequid Hills, would give birth to those rivers of ice so feared by Alpine villagers. Then we'd be in real trouble. Because unless the climate suddenly warmed, they would creep downhill toward the sea, grinding hilltops to rubble, burying forests and towns alike in

an unstoppable slow-motion avalanche which might continue for centuries, even millennia, as they did before, and as the signs all about us attest. Long before this happened, those of us who could would have migrated south to compete for whatever crowded land was still left, or perhaps to occupy new lands created by the steady lowering of the oceans as more and more water was locked up in ice. Think of it—shore frontage on Georges Bank.

All this would have taken so long to come to pass that the beloved place names of Atlantic Canada would have been forgotten by our offspring and even the word Canada would be a lost memory, and scattered groups of wandering hunters would be the only sign that people ever lived here at all.

Takes your mind off your troubles, doesn't it? A mind-boggling scenario, far too big to spin from a failed corn patch or a few snowbanks on the Long Range Mountains, you say. Granted, there is no firm evidence for the return of a real Ice Age. The most that climatologists will say is that the world has undergone a definite cooling trend since the 1950s, accompanied by erratic weather such as Mediterranean snowfalls, failed monsoons and unexpected flooding, and that the toasty summers we had come to regard as normal were an aberration.

Patrick McTaggart-Cowan, former head of the Canadian Meteorological Service, warned in 1974 that Canada should look to its vulnerable transportation network—we have more highways per capita than anyone else in the world—and moreover that we should start worrying about hanging onto southern agricultural land instead of paving it over. And no less an authority than Reid A. Bryson, professor of meteorology and geography at the University of Wisconsin-Madison and advisor to international groups concerned with climate and food production, points out that warm inter-glacials have usually lasted between 8,000 and 12,000 years—and that the present one has already gone on for about 10,800.

Take my advice. Keep an eye on those hills.

—1985

• An Unaccountable Warmth •

Strange, isn't it, how certain moments print themselves so vividly on the mind that for months and years afterward, the merest scent or taste or even sound can bring everything flooding back?

A meal of fish did that to me last night. Nothing special about it—just a mess of winter smelt, the last package left in the freezer from this year's supply. Yet as I sat down to eat the delicious little fish, pan-fried with crisp pork cubes and served with buttered green beans and flaky potatoes, I recalled the experience as if it were yesterday.

The entry in my journal is dated January 16, 1981, the day I went to Jeddore on Nova Scotia's eastern shore to do a workshop at the high school. It was mid-afternoon when we finished. Ordinarily I would have headed straight home, taking the cross-country route north to Truro. Something in the lambent sunshine slanting warmly across the parking lot that day, something about the landscape as it lay shimmering with fresh snow under a cloudless sky, wooed me away. Why not explore a little? It had been a hard day. I could still be home by supper time.

So I drove southwest along the coast, taking the curves at a leisurely pace, admiring the repetition of open ocean, frozen cove, iceworn cliff, humpbacked hill, motionless tree, feeling myself gradually unwind with the road. Suddenly, crossing one of these little bridges so typical of the eastern shore, I spotted five or six black objects far out on the white expanse of an inlet. They looked for a moment like outhouses that had lost their grip on the shore; but I knew they were fishermen's huts.

My first thought was—smelt! Might they have some to sell? I hadn't tasted one in a twelvemonth.... Before I could get a good look, another humpbacked hill intervened and the inlet was lost to view. I would have to slow down and look for a trail of some sort leading through the woods to the huts. Braking slightly, I began to scan the road on that side. Not only did I want some smelt, I hoped to observe how they fished them in this part of the country.

As kids in Newfoundland we had hauled them up through a round hole laboriously chopped with an axe and screened behind a windbreak of fir boughs. The big thing was to know where to cut the hole; the second thing was to keep the water from flooding it before you got the bottom layers chopped all around. With a foot or more of ice you had to gauge it so that at the first jet of water you could knock the final lens of ice out with one or two downward thrusts of the axehead. Otherwise you'd have to worry the last few inches away while gallons of frigid seawater boiled up through one tiny hole.

In the midst of this reverie I spotted three vehicles parked on my side a short ways up the road. Pulling in behind a battered blue pickup, I took a look around. There was a foot-path snaking up the embankment and into the woods. I hauled on my boots and parka and struck out for the huts, which could not be too far away.

In the woods the snow was knee-deep. But on the trail, which was trodden hard from frequent use—though so narrow that if two people met, one of them would have to step aside—the going was good. I met nobody. Judging by the lack of new cutting, the path was an old one, used winter and summer. Perhaps, I mused, Micmacs walked here before the white man came. Likely they had trails like this for all their overland travels, an unmapped network linking each band's ancestral sites for clamming, fishing, egging, hunting, prospecting for flintstones, berrying and burying....

A tree root caught the toe of my boot and sent me sprawling. The low sun flashing between the shaggy trees created a rich tracery of mauve and gold but made it hard to see. I wondered how much farther it was. A clearing opened up ahead; it was only a power line. Another stretch of woods, downhill now, and abruptly the trees were smaller and fewer. I stood on the sloping ice-strewn beach with the shacks not three hundred yards away and the trail running arrow-straight toward them. After a pause to catch my breath I plodded out.

Once within earshot, I yelled a greeting and headed for the nearest hut. Like the rest, it was thrown together of scrap plywood and old two-by-fours covered in heavy plastic and capped with a lean-to roof. Through the open door I saw two men in their sixties sitting across from each other on makeshift benches, concentrating like chess players on a one-by-four-foot rectangle of slushy water at their feet. Each held a short plastic rod built like a miniature surf casting rod but with a tee instead of a reel to wind the line on. They let the tips of their rods angled down, every now and then giving the line a quick little jerk. Their hands were bare and raw but they didn't seem to notice. Each wore a navy blue watch cap, two or three faded mackinaw shirts of indeterminate colours, and heavy wool pants stuffed into patched knee rubbers. I felt conspicuous in my galoshes and dress cords and clean parka.

"How do," said the one on the right cheerfully, without looking up. His ruddy face and thatch of white hair reminded me of pictures I'd seen of Greg Clark. "Where ya from?" smiled the guy on the left. He had sad bloodhound eyes and didn't look a bit like Jimmy Frise.

"Up Truro way," I replied, relieved that they didn't seem to resent my intrusion. "Any luck? I thought I might buy some smelt off you if you had any to spare."

"Wish we had, glad to of," said the white-haired one, lifting his empty hook clear of the water and baiting it with a small chunk of eel that had some skin on one side. "Ralph and me just come," he added, slipping the baited hook with its oblong red sinker and ice-crusted line back down into the hole. "Things'll pick up on the incoming tide, any time now." He glanced about the shack. "Hey, tell you what, why don't you try your hand at it? See that hole over there?" He jabbed a ham of a hand until I saw it. "Nobody's using it."

The next thing I knew he'd fitted me out with rod and line and bait, and shoved an old badminton racquet under my arm. "Badminton racquet?" my face must have said. "To clear away ice," he laughed. "It'll be makin' fast as the sun goes down." I'd forgotten the time. The sun was less than a half hour from setting. I hurried to my unexpected rendevous with the little silvery fish that would school up the pond under my feet when the tide turned. "Drop your line to the bottom, then haul her up a few feet," yelled my host as I baited the hook with already numb fingers and slipped it into the dark water.

"Pay no heed to Joe's advice, fella," came a voice from an adjoining hut. "He never caught a smelt in his life!" My friend Joe cursed him good-naturedly. For a time we all fished in silence. From the western shoreline sawtoothed blue shadows crept out across the level plain of snowy ice, now faded to the colour of old linen. The cloudless dome of the sky deepened from turquoise to indigo. Except for an occasional muffled explosion as the pond adjusted to the cooling air, there was not a sound.

Within five minutes we were all catching fish. The tide had turned. It was like being a kid again. But when my tenth smelt lay wriggling in the snow, I realized that the sun had set, and remembered I still had miles to go. I rose stiffly and reluctantly wound my line on the rod, stripping the ice as I went. My feet tingled with cold as I trudged over to return Joe's gear and to thank them. He and Ralph were busy hand-over-handing smelt after smelt on the ice floor and into a plastic bucket; each had two lines going now. I dropped my ten in too. With my family they wouldn't even make a meal.

As I turned to go, two more fishermen arrived carrying lanterns and lunches. One was bragging loudly about catching ninety dozen the night before and four hundred that morning. I asked whether he still had some to sell.

"Sure thing," he boomed, "how many you need?" Twelve or fifteen pounds, I said. "No problem, my friend." Where did he live, I asked. "You know the Irving storage tanks back a ways toward Jeddore? Well, my house is the one with the red gables, there where the road forks. Got a sign out front says SMELTS FOR SALE. Can't miss 'er!"

Cheered by this news, I thanked him, said so long to Joe and Ralph, and set off back along the trail. The evening breeze was sharp on my cheek. Crossing the pond it was blue dusk, but in the woods it was nearly night. On the hardpacked snow my boots squeaked loudly. Now and then a roosting songbird chided me sleepily. Abruptly a commotion erupted on the trail ahead. Five fellows hove into view, their faces eerily lit by two swinging lanterns, their talk hoarse and studded with hearty oaths. We said hello and passed silently. Moments later their voices were swallowed up in the dusky forest. The Eastern Shore Smelt Fishery Night Shift....

At length I regained the road. Seeing the car was almost a surprise; I had a fey sense of having slipped back in time a century or more. But it was indeed a real automobile, the product of good old Mitsubishi Motors of Japan. A few miles back I found the house of the red gables, where the loud fisherman's aging parents sold me three four-pound bags of frozen smelt for a total of sixteen dollars, a price I was glad to pay, since smelt lose nothing from being frozen.

Driving home through the starry dark, my prize wrapped in a jacket so it wouldn't thaw, I felt as happy as if I had caught the smelt myself. It had been one of those rare afternoons that cozy the mind for years to come. I was basking in the unaccountable warmth of the ice fisherman's Arctic world.

—1982

• A Touch of Wilderness •

W hether it's the wind booming in the big maples outside our bedroom window that rouses us, or the children shouting "Wow! Look at those drifts!"—we don't know. But we wake with a start, knowing we have a real blizzard on our hands.

The kids crowd to the windows. There'll be no school today; there's no road to the school. There's no driveway even. Our car is just a blur in the howling whiteness. And the power is off.

Padding downstairs in the gray light, I'm struck by the silence inside the house. Sounds I never noticed before are suddenly loud in their absence. In the family room Danny's aquarium pump is still, and his goldfish, deprived of their overhead bulb, their sun, hover and stare dazedly out of their cooling world. In the next room I miss the orange eye and soft purr of the freezer, full of our summer garden produce. The fridge stands silent in the kitchen, where wet snow has plastered the windows dark. From the basement there is no comfortable breathing from the hot air furnace, and there will be no rhythmic clacking from the water pump, no blowtorch sound from the propane water heater. In the whole house the only mechanical sound is the clock's ticking.

I find myself liking this silence. It's like the hush of the forest. Even while counting the conveniences we and others will do without during this storm, I savour it. The children don't just savour—they exult. It seems the more isolated and helpless we become the more they enjoy it. Of course the prospect of no school colours their response. Yet there's far more to it than this.

"Daddy, can we have a fire in the fireplace?" They know what to do with a storm. Eagerly the boys fetch wood. Soon we sit circled and warm in the living room, eating breakfast before the crackling yellow flames, leaving the dim kitchen to the already enveloping chill. Our pup Igor eyes the blaze with suspicious sidelong dog glances and keeps a very safe distance. He's never seen an indoor fire before.

The morning passes. Outside, the skies smoke with driven snow, branches toss, and drifts build higher. Like ships at sea each house rides the tempest in isolation with doors and windows battened. On the entire horizon no friendly light or human movement is visible. A touch of wilderness.

At noon I let the fire die down to coals and we grill cheese sandwiches on two old wire toasters. I'm pleased to discover that our token modern fireplace, though too small for spitting a pioneer's roast, can nonetheless serve as a hearth of sorts. With an S-hook made from a coat hanger I can at least hang a pot from the chimney draft lever and boil water for hot chocolate. The sandwiches can't be turned out fast enough. Igor inches closer.

By mid-afternoon the light is already waning. My wife is hooking a rug. The children busy themselves with books and paint and games. TV is never mentioned. Their amity astounds us.

Soon it is time for supper. The blackened pot now serves to heat stew. Again, delicious! Despite my decree not to flush the toilet, water pressure is low; but there's still enough in the pipes for tea. No dishes have been washed since yesterday and if this keeps up we'll be using snow water.

Meanwhile the children have dug out Christmas candles, and I light the handsome kerosene parlour lamp their grandmother gave us. With the small room now suffused in the saffron glow of firelight, lamplight and candlelight, I'm struck by another phenomenon that electrical living has largely eliminated—the play of shadows. They lunge about the walls and ceiling in tall Gothic shapes every time we move the lights or ourselves—the stuff of ghost stories.

One by one, much earlier than usual, gliding carefully with hands cupped before their candles, our children ascend to bed. Later, asleep, their faces wear pleased expressions, as if fair visions are floating in their minds. We feel it too, even as the storm thunders on outside.

In some ways children are wiser than adults. I think they know that this lapse from electrical living is somehow more elemental, more real. To them the Modern Age was simply cancelled for a day while we sat by a cozy campfire, secure from menaces raging without. That such a lapse would very soon hurt us does not prove their instinct wrong. They know that comfort without challenge is also perilous. We reassure ourselves that we conquered the wilderness once and for all, generations ago.

The children in their Palaeolithic souls know better.

—1975

Celebrations

The world is a pomegranate indeed, which God
hath put into man's heart....

Thomas Traherne
Centuries

• The Blue Dory •

The painting I did that day has long since disappeared—sold or given away, I guess. But the circumstances, though ordinary, are fresh in my mind after twenty years.

We were working as summer university students on a forest survey in the Bonavista Peninsula of northeast Newfoundland. Every few weeks we'd shift to another location by truck, train, motor boat, canoe. We lived under canvas, in government camps, sometimes in boarding houses.

When work and weather permitted I'd take my painting gear and tramp to some likely spot and make a sketch. More often than not I scraped the result off the panel in disgust. Yet there were enough successes to keep me trying. Like many young painters, I still imagined that somewhere there waited the perfect landscape, the ideal topography needing only my touch to transform it into a masterpiece. It was years later that I was brought up short by reading Whistler's remark that, when painting outdoors, he first found a comfortable place to sit, then decided what to paint.

One Sunday morning I resolved to paint the headland across the harbour. There was no road to it; I'd need a boat. At this time we were staying in a boarding-house, so I asked our landlady where I might borrow one. Mrs. Walsh glanced up from her dish-washing and regarded me with a quizzical look on her kindly face. After a moment she said: "Why not try Mrs. Rideout just up the road? She has a boat that's never used; tell her I sent you."

Around 10 a.m., packsack and portable easel slung over my shoulder, I rapped on her door. Footsteps sounded along a hallway. The door opened. Before me, blinking a little in the morning light, stood a small, gray-haired woman in her sixties, evidently dressed for church. Her blue eyes flicked over my attire, then rivetted on my face. "Mrs. Rideout?" I asked.

"Yes?"

"Ma'am," I began, "I'm with the forest survey...." Her stare was making me fidget. "We're staying at Mrs. Walsh's, and she suggested that you might lend me your boat for a few hours."

"That so? What for, may I ask?" Her eyes still measured me.

I explained.

"You paint on the Sabbath?" She stressed the last word.

"Sometimes," I felt my scalp prickling with anger.

"Don't you ever attend church?"

"Sure, but I like to paint, too, and I only have the weekends. However, I don't need your boat badly enough to beg for it, Mrs. Rideout." I turned to go.

"Wait," she said. "I guess it will be all right... this once. But you'll have to take very good care of it, and return it promptly at, let me see, three this afternoon, without fail. And be sure to moor it properly." Her manner softened as she pointed across the road to the wharf. "There it is, the small blue dory next to the white motor boat. I keep it moored off rather than haul it up; when they're out of water they dry out and get leaky, you know. Arthur—that's my husband—always took good care of his boats."

More instructions were given. I even promised not to get paint on it. I noted that she watched me all the way to the wharf. It was a little annoying. I still considered dropping the whole idea.

But when I saw the boat up close my doubts vanished. It was a lovely little dory, tight and trim and painted sky blue inside and out; the work of an expert builder. I untied it fore and aft, stowed my gear, unshipped the oars and set out.

The harbour was as calm as a clock. Gradually as I rowed, the boat's wake and the dipping of the oars sent out ripples that spread and criss-crossed in complex mackerel patterns on the glassy surface. By now the sun was burning through the morning mists. The air tasted like chilled champagne. Somewhere a sheep bleated, a dog barked, children laughed. Church bells began to chime; first the slow deep notes of one church, then the high rapid notes of another. I rowed steadily on. My shoulders began to ache. Now and then I glanced ahead to see how far the headland was away and to check my course.

After about an hour I rounded a rocky point, chose a likely landing place and drew into a small cove. The tide was rising. I pulled the dory ashore and tied it to a tree root.

The view had less to offer than I'd expected. A rocky path led me uphill through wind-stunted balsam fir bearded with pale green lichens to an old graveyard where waist-high aster and goldenrod all but hid the stones. Nearby was a rectangular depression half-filled with rubble and rotting boards; a church, perhaps.

By now I was getting hungry. Coming back down the steep path, I was struck by the high view of the boat in the little cove; blue dory, yellow kelp, dark trees. Nice sky reflections. That's good, I thought. Even better than the headland. Yes.

In some excitement I fished out my cheese sandwich and thermos of tea from the knapsack, set up the easel, laid out my painting tackle and commenced working.

For once the picture fairly painted itself. When I finished two hours later, the sky had clouded over and the wind was breezing up from the southwest and raising a lop on the harbour. Rowing back in the teeth of it was hard. Toward the end the dory was taking in some water; I had to cover the painting with my jacket.

I restored the dory carefully to its moorings as the widow had instructed and bailed out the water that had sloshed in. My watch said ten to three. While thanking her, I showed her the painting so she'd at least know how I'd spent my time. She invited me to stand it against a kitchen chair while she made us a cup of tea. Once the tea was served, we sat for a time and studied the picture. It crossed my mind that she might wish to have it. In those days I gave away a lot of pictures. She seemed to like it all right; but I sensed it saddened her, too. She said nothing, seemed to be lost in thought. After a while I thanked her again and left with the painting.

A fortnight later our party moved on. I never saw the widow again. As it turned out, 'The Blue Dory' was the best thing I did that summer. Yet for a good while her negative response troubled me.

Then one day a year later I ran into a fellow I knew from that community, and asked his opinion why. "Oh," he laughed, "that's not too hard to figure, if you know the background. When she and Arthur were courting he used to take her places in a dory; picnics, trouting, berry-picking—that sort of thing. Then came years of hard work in the lumberwoods and at sea. He was away a lot. They lost their only son in the war. After Arthur retired a few years back he built her that special dory, thinking, I suppose, to recapture something of those bygone years. Even painted it her favourite colour. But before he could take her for a single trip in it, the poor man suffered a stroke and died. That was four springs ago."

"Ever since then she's treated that boat like a china doll, checking on it a dozen times a day the first few months after he died. Always scraping and repainting it. Never letting anyone use it. At the same time, she stopped going anywhere but church. Her friends were getting really worried about her, trying to draw her out. Until this summer."

"Oh?"

"Yes, it was the queerest thing. She seemed to snap out of it. It happened about the time she lent you the dory. Did you know that you were the first person she ever lent it to?"

"No. Why would she pick me?"

"Who knows? People do things for the strangest reasons. But some of the older people think they understand—Mrs. Walsh, for instance. She claims you are the spitting image of Arthur when he was young."

—1979

• Train Ride •

It's not often I save empty litterbags. Or full ones, for that matter. And there was nothing special about this one; all the inscription said was:

CN

LITTERBAG

SAC À REBUT

NOT FOR CIGARETTES

PAS DE CIGARETTES

But here it is lying folded in my file a year later, all scribbled over in black ink. For I took an unexpected train trip last spring, and found it such a nice experience that I had to get some of it down in writing. The litterbag was the only paper handy at the time.

Now this isn't a sponsored piece for CN. Nor is it meant as a bit of nostalgia on the joys of train travel. No; it's about the unexpected pleasures of renewing an acquaintance with locomotives, of seeing the land and the people from a different angle. It's also about the luxury of being a detached observer—relieved for once of the need to steer, able for once to concentrate on something more relaxing than the preservation of life and limb.

As it happened I wasn't bent on pleasure. My mission was simply to get from Truro, N.S., to Sackville, N.B., to fetch our car, which we'd been forced to leave in a garage there two weeks before. The train was just a means. I even resented the time it would take.

It's not that trains are all that slow. But no matter how fast they roll, the passengers seem to suffer a cerebral slowdown. How can one maintain the mental rush when there's no wheel to grip, no highway to scan, no gas gauge to eye, no expensive noises to listen for?

So finding myself in motion with nothing to do, I began to unwind. It didn't take long. I just looked out the window. In a motor car this is curiously hard to do, even for passengers. A blindness sets in. All but the bizarre and spectacular become invisible. Not so by train. Looking down from the high wide windows, the first thing that struck me was the startling freshness of everything. Familiar objects like rocks and weeds fairly jumped out at me. It was like getting outdoors again after being sick in bed for two weeks. Or like studying the back yard through binoculars. Of course novelty had a lot to do with this. And the fact that it was spring may have sharpened the effect.

Even so, reading my litterbag notes now, I wonder why I take the train so seldom. Habit, I guess. Too bad. Maybe the rising cost of gasoline will cool our love affair with the automobile enough to make us realize what we're missing.

At 1:05, after some tentative jolts, we start at last. From under the wheels gray pigeons with peacock necks and ruby eyes skitter and flap out of danger. For a moment we thread a dark canyon of brown boxcars stippled with railway hieroglyphs, then break out into blinding May sunshine. Glimpse of hazy mauve clouds banked high to the south. Abruptly the buildings and boxcars fall away and we are crossing the level Acadian dykelands that border Cobequid Bay, a patchwork of green and brown rectangles dotted with black and white cattle dozing in the unaccustomed heat. Off to the left, like shiny beetles, a stream of southbound autos descends the ramp from the Trans Canada...gas guzzlers, high on horsepower, low on passengers. Up ahead our whistle blows, inundating the countryside with that inimitable, wind-baffled organ note....

Always the whistle gets me. No other sound quite equals it—except perhaps the midnight bawl of a departing ocean liner. The oldtime steam whistle had the best timbre; but the air horn of a modern diesel locomotive is not bad, especially when mellowed by distance. When you're on board it's even sweeter.

A slight rise and we are off the flats and into a dark spruce forest fringed with wild rhodora in frothy pink bloom and broken by occasional cutovers greening with new growth. Pin cherries are in late flower. The sun, streaming through the south windows, gets too hot so I move to the north side of the coach, which today is nearly empty. Now the engine is reaching top speed. Open fields flash by, then a power line, a brook, a cluster of houses, a high brown gravel bank. Plunging into the dark woods again, we charge through tangles of blown timber from last February's gale. Suddenly a clattering orange-black blur of boxcars fills the windows on my side; then we leap into space on a steel bridge 60 feet above the Trans Canada, a bridge Sir Sandford Flemming first built of wood a century before....

Sir Sandford wanted steel from the outset, but the budget for this stretch of the Intercolonial couldn't stand it. He also wanted to run the line straight north here instead of looping west to service the iron mines at Londonderry. He lost out on this too. "The Grecian Bend," his critics called it.

Railroads boast so much more history. With highways it's altogether different. At least it seems so. The politics are there of course, but not the heroics. Everything seems so mechanical and mediocre. I find it hard to imagine anyone writing a national bestseller about the building of the Trans Canada, or even an apt title for it. *The Last Cubic Yard?*

Approaching the lower slopes of the thousand-foot Cobequid Hills, we commence to labour on the grade. Wheels and trucks squeak, sounding vaguely like a wind orchestra tuning up. Acrid smell of diesel fumes, not unlike oldtime coal smoke. Slowly we glide through glades of wind-stunted maple, beech and yellow birch into Londonderry Station. Irish farmers settled hereabouts after the Acadian expulsion, long before the iron was discovered. Steadily we climb, mounting the worn-down teeth of these onetime Rockies of the East—three times older than the Western peaks and once as high....

It is easy to forget, purring along our smooth asphalt highways with their manicured rights-of-way, what obstacles the builders of our transport systems have to overcome. Travelling by train one can see those obstacles up close. One would almost think the Land meant us to stay put—so extravagantly has she strewn the way with deeps and cliffs and quagmires. Nowhere is this more obvious in the Maritimes than in the Cobequid Hills, which cross mainland Nova Scotia like an east-west wall. And, like a wall they barred the railroad builders from taking the more direct route from Moncton to Halifax, forcing them to push the rails eastward and eastward until they found a chink, a gate. This gate was the Wentworth Valley—in ancient times part of the streambed of a mighty river flowing off the Atlantic Upland out through present-day Halifax harbour and on to its mouth on the edge of the continental shelf a hundred miles south.

Mysterious stop on a siding. Quiet, abstracted voices muffled by other sounds. Exploding out of nowhere, the Halifax-bound express roars past. Another jolt and we resume our ascent. Soon we are high enough to look down on Folly Lake, flashing like a turquoise brooch on the bosom of the pass. Now the train picks up speed as it descends to the Oxford Lowlands, which spread west and north like a rumpled quilt patterned with pea-green fields and spiky woodlots. To the south the mountains recede into blue haze. Northward, across the Strait, Prince Edward Island is a dim presence. Soon the rhythmic clackety-clack of wheel on track lulls me to sleep—a luxury I can't afford when driving. Just as I drop off I glimpse a white-haired man standing in the spring sunshine contemplating his garden.

"Next stop Springhill!" I wake with a start to see the conductor making his way hand-over-hand down the unsteady aisle. Slowing now, we slide through sombre stands of spruce into open sunny glades of red pine sprinkled with birch and aspen, sure signs of forest fires in the past, and typical of the outskirts of most larger towns in Atlantic Canada, especially mining towns....

Thinking back now, I recall that at this point a man and his wife and three teen-aged youths, all in their best attire, arose and nervously awaited their stop. But the train took its time, as if the engineer wished to wheel softly over the sealed tombs of so many coal miners who met their doom in the black shafts and rooms below us. Finally the five had to sit down again. But at last the grimy red station, casting broad shadows from its pagoda-like eaves, loomed to one side.

"Taxi?" Eagerly the family climbs in; doors slam, back wheels spit gravel, and they are gone. Stupidly I wonder if they are related to Anne Murray.

"'Board!" Lurch. Picking up speed. Hum of powerful engine up ahead. Creak of roof, squinch and screek of couplings, clack of wheels. Inrush of outside sounds whenever the doors are opened. A young man with long hair enters cradling a worn guitar under his arm. Presently he tunes the worn guitar; and, gazing out the window, picks out a gentle ballad....

The music made me muse on other trains in other places, especially the now-extinct 'Bullet' snaking along the coastal plain of western Newfoundland with the jade-green Atlantic pounding the shore on my left and the cloud-capped Long Range Mountains glowering on my right, and, at the other end of the car, someone squeezing Irish melodies from an accordion.

Or standing in the raw sooty wind between the cars at night, nearing Christmas and home, blinking against the coal-smoke and trying to catch another glimmer of the flat-roofed mountains through rafts of scudding cloud, printing the moonlit beauty of the spruce bogs on my mind for another time.

Before I knew it, we were out on the Tantramar Marshes and the conductor was shouting "Next stop Sackville!" and it was over.

Trudging up the steep hill from the station to Main Street, I felt a bit down. At the garage they had my car all ready. I paid my bill, thanked them, got in, and headed home.

The return trip was unusually dull.

—1977

• Gander Bay Boat •

*I*n the early morning chill the rising sun floodlights a rosy mist on the *river. Somewhere among the aspen islands a kingfisher rattles its cry. You've risen at dawn and, with your Newfoundland guide, have reached the salmon pool early. Now he has deftly positioned the canoe near the top where you just saw the salmon breach. You cast across the riffle made by that submerged gray boulder. The fly lands delicately, then drifts past where the fish should be.*

If you fish for Atlantic salmon on Newfoundland's deeper west coast streams like the Humber or Serpentine, you're likely to do so from a dory. The dory is a lovely craft on the ocean, yet on a river it looks somehow out of place, like a puffin on a millpond. On other Newfoundland rivers you'll even see small trap-skiffs, the cod fisherman's workhorse.

But if you fish the Gander on the Island's northeast coast you'll cast from a sleek craft which was most likely built by your guide or one of his uncles or grandfathers. At first sight you might think this craft ungainly. It looks like a cross between a skiff and an Old Town Maine canoe—with the canoe genes dominant. But the image of ungainliness will fade when you see it at work on its native river in rough water or high wind, or freighting two forty-five-gallon drums of gasoline and three passengers through shallow rock-strewn channels. Then you'll begin to appreciate what the designers had in mind. They developed it specifically for this river, and now it's known all over Newfoundland and Labrador as the 'Gander Bay Boat'.

...The fly makes its tantalizing circuit without event. You cast again and again across the riffle, savouring the suspense. How could he resist?

Maybe he's moved away? The sun attains treetop height, spangling the riverbed with amber and violet shadows. Your guide grins and rolls a cigarette and you reel in and light up too, sitting in the canoe in the morning sunshine and talking of salmon and rivers and boats....

The craft is twenty-three feet long, four feet wide amidships, and about eighteen inches deep. Except for the nails it is strictly a local forest product—ribbed with tough bendable black spruce, planked with lighter fir, keeled with the durable tamarack or juniper. The bow has a cuddy or covered space to shelter rope and gear. Usually the forward thwart has a high-backed, padded seat for sportsmen. The stern widens from the keel to a small triangle for mounting an outboard motor.

Purists might object to the motor; but they haven't poled and paddled the thirty miles upriver from the Bay to Glenwood. My father made his first such trip in 1919 when he was fifteen. Before the highway came in 1966, Glenwood, being on the trans-island railway, was their only link with the outside world. He made that trip with Micmac guide Jim John in an eighteen-foot cedar canoe and it took them two days. Although roads have reduced the volume of freight and passenger business, Glenwood is still the main pickup point for sportsmen. Today the trip takes only a couple of hours and outboards fit these boats as saddles fit horses. They should, because when outboards appeared in Newfoundland in the 1920s—my father's brother had the first on the Gander—the canoe builders lengthened and rebalanced their craft to accommodate a motor. Cedar canoes were too temperamental for the workhorse role, and poling is backbreaking and slow. Today the boat looks naked without its *Johnson* or *Evinrude* or *Mercury* and the art of poling is still very much alive. So much for the purist.

...Taking his pole, the riverman lifts his light anchor and lets the canoe drift down to a new position. Now the warming sun is sweeping the mists into odd corners of the riverscape. Your smoke over, you change flies and survey the pool. Once more the line snakes out, settling the lure as soft as thistledown....

After a week's fishing on the Gander, you'll find the canoes are beginning to grow on you. You'll begin to perceive nuances of design —a more graceful sweep of gunwale, a longer cuddy, a more rakish prow. You may even wish these boats were less awkward to transport, so you could take one home.

..."Cast a bit further out, ol' man," murmurs your guide in his Devon burr. You do—and the fly detonates a quicksilver explosion of water as the

salmon arcs into the sunlight and streaks off downstream, trying furiously to shake the fly from its jaw while the reel sings the song you love....

That's your Atlantic salmon.

And that's your Gander Bay boat.

—*1975*

• Weedwatch •

The afternoon was hot and humid, the ramrod-straight highway interminably dull. As I drove on, a drowsiness stole over me. Absently I looked for an excuse to shake it off. Then up ahead I spotted an interesting clump of roadside flowers I thought I recognized. Gratefully I stopped, flicked on my flashers, and climbed the bank to get a closer look.

Their small creamy paper-like flowers and silvery foliage readily identified the plants as *Anaphalis*, the Pearly Everlasting or Live-Forever. By no means rare in our region, it has a remarkable feature that makes it memorable for me. An elderly widow opened my eyes to this when she showed me a lovely bouquet of *Anaphalis* her husband had plucked for her the week he died—seventeen years before. They looked quite fresh. No wonder the pioneers stuffed pillows with them, I thought, feeling their stiff, papery blooms and silvery foliage.

Moments later I climbed back behind the wheel. Thanks to this roadside weed, I felt relaxed and alert as I resumed my journey. It was better than a cup of coffee. Maybe a cup of steeped *Anaphalis* would have been better still; but so far I've been content to just look. For me, weed-watching has restored some of the lost pleasures of driving.

Now once upon a time, I am told, automobile trips were fun. In those innocent years before death toll tallies were kept, when low horsepower and deep ruts precluded high speeds, they tell me the scenery was the thing.

It's true that trunk highways are not meant for sightseeing. Side roads are for that. Unfortunately, once we acquire the habit of travel blindness, our perceptions are dulled no matter what class of road we travel. And it seems that the better our highways are built, the duller they are to drive.

So, while I wait for highway engineers to start calculating formulas to keep motorists alert as well as alive from Point A to Point B, I've been devising my own strategies. The *Anaphalis* incident typifies my method. I expect some ridicule. Even birdwatchers of long standing endure a certain stigma. Yet they enjoy a certain prestige, if not notoriety, for being able to name a three-toed wood-pecker at ten paces with seven-power binoculars in one hand and Peterson's *Field Guide* in the other—and standing still, at that. However, compared to identifying the Evening Primrose or Joe Pye Weed at a hundred feet and sixty miles an hour this is child's play. Prestige may be slow in coming; but the potential is there.

Certainly the roadside flowers are there. Despite the best efforts of our departments of agriculture and of highways, legions of them keep invading the neat prescription swards of clover and grass. Though I sympathize with the farmer who sees swarms of lupines or Jimson weed threatening his crops and his cattle, I can't help but rejoice in those hardy and mostly harmless plants that venture to decorate our main highways—volunteers for ecological diversity when monocultures are in vogue.

The easiest way to begin roadside weed-watching is to forget trying to put name-tags on the plants you spot. Just enjoy them en masse for their colours and textures. Fortunately most of them grow in large clumps and many have distinctive hues. Thus one can avoid complicated handbooks and risky stops. Later, field checks and forays into books can fill in the blanks about their names and habits and such. That's the really interesting part. Soon you'll be as hooked as any squint-eyed stamp collector. Soon you'll know them just by colour and by time of flowering. Plants are quite punctual about when they bloom.

Anyway, here (for the doubtful) is a sampling from my proposed *Unscientific Primer for Roadside Weed Freaks.*

MAY
Silent explosions of frothy white: Indian Pear and Mountain-ash.

JUNE
Rose-purple blush on barrens and bogs: Wild Rhododendron; cool blue in damp meadows: Blue-Flag Iris.

JULY
Magenta flush across acres of wasteland: Fireweed or Large
Willow-Herb; spangle of gold in dry ditches: Hawkweed,
Ragwort, Black-eyed Susan.

AUGUST
Silver-green of Pearly Everlasting (who we've met); first golds
of goldenrod...and so on.

Not to mention constellations of dandelions and buttercups,
drifts of daisies and yarrow, thickets of thistle and elder, cattail
swamps alive with red-winged blackbirds, lakes bobbing with rafts
of pond lily, swales thorny with wild rose. It's enough to bring out
the poet in anyone.

And I still haven't written September and October—the two
best months of all. First come the real harbingers of autumn, the
purple asters and late-blooming goldenrods. Though both abound
throughout the Atlantic area, in my mind these native plants are
inseparably associated with sun-steeped, windless October
afternoons in New Brunswick, when the hardwood hills throb with
crackling reds and yellows under Van Gogh skies of cobalt blue, and
only the sleepy dirge of crickets and the hum of late-working bees
disturbs the immense, dry hush.

This hobby gets to you.

Is it the imminence of winter that tinges such memories with
regret? For as the bees well know, those halcyon days are numbered.
Soon, chill November rains will quench the fires. Volleys of bitter
sleet will thresh the withered stalks and patter on fallen and faded
leaves. Then motoring will be a different matter indeed, requiring
other stratagems.

Still, in their short summer lifetime these hosts of wild roadside
flowers can brighten drab green miles for motorists who care to look,
and may help restore some of the simple pleasures of automobile
travel. Long after the holiday bumper stickers have worn off in
winter's dirty slush, their friendly colours sing in the heart.

—1975

"A Steady Little Business"
• Weatherby's Hardware •
of Truro, Nova Scotia

For twenty years now I have had the good fortune of taking my hardware business, small as it is, to an old Truro establishment where they know my name and where the owner, Hartley C. Weatherby, always makes time to chat. It's the kind of place, moreover, where waiting one's turn simply means more time to enjoy the soothing hum of the aquarium and the antics of the guppies and tetras, a better chance to study the display of dark old tools resting from their labours on the high white walls, to count the astounding diversity of canine and feline amusements and accoutrements, and to revel in the sculptural exuberance of kettles, colanders and casseroles, of hammers, screwdrivers and lamp chimneys, of bicycles, skates, clocks, orange-squeezers and the latest gadget for coring an apple.

My twenty years are but a moment as time is reckoned in old Maritime towns like Truro. Weatherby's Hardware at 590 Prince Street, Truro's main thoroughfare, goes back twice as long, to the year 1941, when Hartley acquired the three-storey building which three generations of Truronians had known as 'The Market'. He was then twenty-five. For three-and-a-half years before that he had run a small hardware business in rented premises (formerly Phinney's, a tinsmith) just up the street. And before that he worked six years as a delivery boy and clerk for Crockers, a large hardware and china business uptown on Inglis Street.

After fifty-four years in retail hardware—in 1981 he won the Maritime Wholesale Hardware Association's *Golden Hammer* award for fifty years in the business—one might think Hartley gets tired of it. At times perhaps he does. But to watch him—a trim, balding white-haired man of sixty-nine whose step is quick and whose movements are precise—one would never guess. To his doctor and others who urge him to slow down, he quotes the wag who said, "I can work just as hard as ever—I just get tired quicker."

But he's no workaholic. Back in August when I approached him about this interview and suggested some evening, he was agreeable but added, "This is an awful time for baseball, you know— I'm out just about every evening to a game." I settled instead for a couple of quiet noon hours in the store, with me asking questions between customers and scribbling notes as he served. It was apparent that Hartley blended work and play seamlessly. And this, with his outgoing nature and good business sense, probably explains the longevity of Weatherby's Hardware.

Certainly the premises—essentially a long narrow space jam-packed with merchandise and overflowing in summer with bicycles under repair and in winter with skates being sharpened—are not in style. The building itself is at least as old as Confederation. The real attraction is a certain quality of individual service, of attention to detail, that he and his son Gordon bring to each customer. This was evident each time a customer entered during our talk. Hartley would bustle to meet their need—a hammer handle, some bolts, a candy thermometer, some fly stickers, a flea collar, a duplicate key. Always there was a pleasant remark or two, a helpful suggestion or explanation, and, if he knew the person, a short conversation.

"And how've you been keeping?" he says, wrapping their parcel with brown manila paper off a roll and breaking the white cotton twine deftly with his forefinger.

"Oh, pretty good. Can't complain."

"That's good. See you again...."

I asked him about Truro in the old days. "Well," he said, "back then we delivered everything, you know, and people kind of expected it. Truro had a good many motor cars of course, but even at thirty cents a gallon not many could afford the gas to run them. Summertime we made a lot of deliveries by bicycle. In the winter we would use a horse and sloven." A slow smile curved the corners of his mouth.

"One day," he said, "a woman dressed in black came in and wanted two tap washers. A tap washer is only about the size of a nickel, so I put them in a little paper bag. But when I handed them to her, she asked would I mind delivering them. Said she was on her way to a funeral and didn't want to carry them." He chuckled. "We delivered."

It helps to know your customers. Born in nearby Lower Truro and a lifelong resident of Truro, he possesses an enormous fund of knowledge about Truronians in general and about his customers' likes and dislikes in particular. He left school at fifteen to help his father Henry in the landscaping business, which despite the Depression was doing well. Although he promised to go back to school in the fall, he only attended for one day. Within seven years he had his own business, and at twenty-five his own building. And at the end of the war he had the chance to buy out Crockers on Inglis. He declined. "I had a steady little business here, a friendly little business—why move?" is how he puts it.

The bicycles have always intrigued me. I asked if he had been a cyclist in his youth. "No, nothing like that; I always liked to work with bicycles," he said, lingering on the "bi" like a Southerner. "When I opened my first shop I just put a sign in the window and it grew from that. Back then I never bought and sold them—couldn't afford to." After moving to 590 Prince he had the funds and space to do both, and now carries a full line plus accessories. Weatherby's Hardware has long since become Truro's leading bicycle hospital, serving not only its own customers, but patients from Zellers, K-Mart and Canadian Tire as well. They even fix sulky wheels at times. In summer it's common for the lights to burn late in the little shop out back as Hartley or Gordon perform major surgery on a dislocated derailleur or a fractured wheel. Their only hope against the flood of bikes is to seize every spare moment, to stock plenty of parts and to work swiftly and surely. One of the small pleasures in life is to watch Hartley or Gordon change a tire and tube in minutes with their bare hands.

Bikes aren't the only things Hartley repairs. "You wouldn't believe," says Gordon's wife Joan, who also helps in the store, "the number of old ladies who come in with the elements burned out of their electric tea kettles." Hartley smiles as he recalls one who brought him her purse to fix. The clasp was broken on one side. He repaired it at no charge and she went away content. A week later she returned, set her purse on the counter and announced, "Mr.

Weatherby, one good turn deserves another—would you mind fixing the clasp on the other side now?"

When red and yellow leaves start collecting along the curbs on Prince Street, the bicycles disappear in Weatherby's and mounds of hockey skates pile up on the wooden floor along the counters. Father and son then spend long hours at the emery wheel by the woodstove out back, goggled against the bright, gushing sparks as they hone tired blades. Weatherby's also sells skates. They know that nothing is quite so irritating as new boots that pinch or chafe. So they take pains to assure each buyer a good fit. One young lady who bought a pair of size five *Star* skates years ago claimed they were too tight and wanted half a size larger. After years of fitting skates Hartley knew better, but he had no five-and-a-halfs in stock to prove his point. So he promised that on his next buying trip to the factory in Dartmouth he would bring her back a pair of five-and-a-halfs. Unfortunately, the company had none in stock either. But so sure was he that the pinch was psychological, he had them engrave "one-half" after the "five" on the bottom plate of each. "When the girl tried them on," he said, "she declared them a perfect fit."

When Gordon first mentioned 'The Coffee Gang' I pictured a band of desperados. I was surprised to learn that his father was a founding member. It turned out to be just a club where local businessmen and friends gather morning and afternoon to shoot the breeze. The amazing part is that they have been doing this since 1945. "A bunch of us took to having coffee in the snack bar at Layton's Grocery back when Frank Yould came back from overseas and started in business," explained Hartley. "We've been doing it ever since; different fellas, of course, but the same custom. At times we've had as many as twenty-two, other times only two or three show up. Some current members are Bob Jones of R.H. Jones; Eric McDade, insurance salesman; Ozzie Henderson, commercial traveller; Dr. Roy Davis the dentist and Terry Honey of the *Truro Daily News*. Oh, yes—and I musn't forget Ken Lewis and Tom Frazer, who've only been with us since around 1962...." Nowadays the Coffee Gang hangs out at the Maritimer Restaurant just up the street. Sometimes they amble over to the shop for a taste of the creamy dark chocolate fudge Hartley's wife Margie makes. Having tasted it myself I can understand why the club has endured so long.

Concluding the interview, I asked Hartley whether he'd ever considered moving to another town, setting up business somewhere else. He smiled and shook his head. "No," he said softly, "Truro is all I know.... I guess you might say I found everything I always wanted right here. Hockey and ball, and, above all, friends. To me, friends are the Number One thing in life. If you have friends and health, then everything else falls into place."

—1985

• My Rediscovery of Bicycling •

For me, bicycling to work began as a protest and ended as a passion.

My protest was against the steady rain of bad news about rising pollution and dwindling energy, and against the thought that we Atlantic Canadians—of all people—should find ourselves stuck to the same energy tar baby as the rest of North America.

Looking back over my first six years as a commuter cyclist, I wonder why I didn't leave the car home long before. For as kids we lived on bicycles from spring through fall. But something happened. We grew up and went away and got jobs and cars, and we began to imagine that bikes were kids' stuff. And later on we settled down to mortgages and TV and overeating and oversmoking, and presently the solar plexus sagged, the lungs shrank, the sternum caved in— and there we were, prime candidates for a coronary the next time we shovelled snow or dug a rose bush.

So my rediscovery of the bicycle was a near thing. Oh, I had flirted briefly with a one-speed, one-ton, sit-up model when I lived in St. John's in the early 1960s and couldn't afford a motor car. (I can't afford one now either; I just had more sense then.)

But there was no passion in that affair. I just rode doggedly to and from work, feeling conspicuous because so few other adults rode bicycles. And the winds blew constantly. When it was fine they blew from the west and when it was dirty (which was often) they blew from the east. Along the streets the poor trees were gnarled and prematurely bald from all that buffeting, and I began to fear the same fate.

And the hills! Anyone who has climbed or even examined photos of those perpendicular streets linking the waterfront of St.John's with its Upper Levels knows what I mean. Picturesque, yes; but to a one-speed cyclist such slopes are murder. Even the goats and sheep who (it is said) originally laid out that city's thoroughfares had the sense to cling to the contours.

And worst of all, the jeers. At that time the average St. John's youth seemed to think that any adult who rode a bicycle had to be some kind of nut. A gang of them even slung rocks at me once. But that was fifteen years, one motor bike and several cars ago.

What restored me my senses was an article by Harry Cunningham in a newsletter put out by the Manitoba government in 1970. I wish I could find it now because it was both funny and practical. After reading it I resolved to buy a lightweight ten-speed bicycle.

That was the easiest part.

It is positively shameful, the number of excuses an otherwise normal person can dream up to avoid so simple a thing as riding a bike a few miles to and from work. One would almost think Stephen Leacock was right after all when he said (of fresh air and exercise):

Don't bother with either of them. Get your room full of good air,
then shut up the windows and keep it. It will keep for years.
Anyway, don't keep using your lungs all the time. Let them rest.
As for exercise, if you have to take it, take it and put up with it.

I had the devil's own job overcoming such procrastinations as "Mmmm... looks like rain today; better take the car," or "Oh, oh... got a sore throat again... might be wise to leave the bike home until it clears up...," or "Feelin' kinda tired this morning; guess I'll take the easy way for once."

Of course there were legitimate excuses, too: foul weather, groceries to pick up, a package to deliver, out-of-town business, company coming early for supper. Still, it was amazing how often the car was taken for granted and unthinkingly used, day after day, for errands and chores which, with a little planning, could be grouped and just as easily accomplished in one trip.

The family and co-workers soon adjusted. About the only other problem in those first weeks was fear of B.O. As H. Cunningham put it, "All you need is a forty-five gallon drum of your favourite deodorant." Scrubbing off the sweat in the office washroom did cause some kidding and nervous glances for a while.

Now I feel cheated when I have to leave the bike home. Now setting off to work in the morning is a pleasure and travelling home a delight. The elements and essences that windshields isolate us from —wind, rain, scents, bugs, sounds, heat, and cold—are more real. For the price of three weeks' groceries my life has taken on a new dimension.

Take wind, for instance. Wind in the face and in the hair. How long has it been since you've come swooping silently and effortlessly down a long hill, making your own breeze without the aid of an internal combustion engine? Not since childhood?

Of course wind can be discouraging too. On my own seven-mile route, in fact, fine weather usually means a stiff breeze against me on the way home, especially when the moon is tugging the cold Fundy tides in over the warm mud flats. Sometimes I curse this relentless wind. It reminds me of my St. John's route.

But once the leg muscles strengthen and the lungs expand and the heart regains its natural stamina, the wind can seem more like a friendly adversary, testing your mettle. Now and then it will even relent and help you along—what seamen call a free wind. And in time you learn to predict its moods.

I have to laugh at radio announcers and their endless prattle about sun and warmth, as if rain were the ultimate disaster and a sunny weekend the ultimate good, as if all their listeners were mariners or farmers or airline pilots. The average listener, sheltered as he or she is by roofs and walls of one sort or another, certainly has no need of so much weather information.

Since taking up bicycling, however, I've been paying the DJs' weather chatter more heed and keeping a watchful eye on the too-red dawn, the menacing nimbus at noon, the mackerel skies and mares' tails, the fair-weather sunsets, the ringed moon. And my guesses are getting better than theirs. When I drove a car every day I hardly noticed.

Then there are the smells, odours, aromas, fragrances and stinks that seldom penetrate an auto interior. About the only two that get through are pig manure and run-over skunk—and then only faintly. But wheeling through the open air is a whole new experience for the olfactory apparatus. In quick succession the nostrils recoil from the hot breath of a diesel truck, wrinkle at barnyard odours, savour restaurant aromas of fresh coffee and french fries, rejoice at the fragrances of new-mown grass, quiver at the factory stench of rendered fat or burnt rubber. And one makes intriguing discoveries.

For instance, night air magnifies and sharpens nuances. One night, pedalling along a country lane and enjoying the cool-warm-cool alternation of air layers with their mingled and fading daytime smells, I picked up the perfume of wild roses, followed, an instant later, by the reek of a cesspool. The contrast heightened the effect, just as it does with colour.

Cyclists also hear more. Until I took up the bicycle I never realized how full of birdsong the roadsides are. Even the sound of a person walking can silence most of them. On a bicycle you hear them before they hear you. How many mornings and evenings, driving my car, have I missed the bobolink's exuberant matins in this green meadow, the hermit thrush's modest evensong in that shadowy woodlot?

One sound I will never forget. Riding down a country road one dark night, my eleven-year-old son and I were chased by a runaway Holstein bull whose hoofbeats still echo in my mind. Holstein bulls have a deserved reputation for meanness. This one would have done well in the arena in Madrid or Seville; the bullfighter Belmondo would have liked him. To lose him we had to pedal like hell, and when at last the pounding of his hooves subsided behind us and we felt it safe to halt, we were so scared and relieved that we laughed our fool heads off in the darkness. Now I'd almost like to race him again.

To this catalogue of cycling delights I should add the sense of taste. Last summer, at a halfway place where I often stop to rest, I came upon a patch of wild strawberries. The place is pleasant enough as it is. There are cool breezes off the water. At ebb tide one can watch seagulls and sandpipers probing the chocolate-coloured mud flats for tidbits. Across the bay loom the low blue Cobequid Mountains, three times older than the upstart Rockies. Down the bay one can see past the mouth of the Shubenacadie and on out toward the open tide-churned Fundy waters whose restless energy may one day light our homes and power our mills.

As if all this were not enough, I found this patch of berries; not wild ones, exactly, but tame ones gone wild and better for it. It was a sultry afternoon and I was hot and thirsty. Hidden as they were down among knee-high timothy and wild carrot and vetch, I nearly missed them. The glint of scarlet gave them away. Gratefully I hand-over-handed the cool luscious fruit into my mouth. My bike stood nearby. A breeze came up, grass swished, aspen leaves pattered, birds warbled, a bee droned past.

A summer moment to hoard against the winter solstice.

Winter, to come right down to it, is the bicyclist's only real problem. Even if a two-wheeled vehicle could safely cope with snow and ice, few cyclists would care to brave our sub-zero temperatures. But as long as the roads are bare it can be done. Just as the members of Polar Bear clubs learn to endure their January dip through the ice, so there are hardy souls who cycle nearly all winter, encased in thermal underwear and fleece-lined mittens and boots. Some even wear electric socks. I may try that. It would extend the biking season by two or three whole months!

Even if I don't go that far, I'm glad I rediscovered bicycling and made it a habit. Of course the sport had always been popular; since the time when Baron Karl von Drais trundled out his prototype, the *Hobby-Horse*, in 1816. But never more so than now. Bicycles began to outsell motor cars in North America several years back. This does not mean, however, that our streets will soon look like those of Hong Kong, with bicycles crowding cars off. Most of our cyclists are under twenty-five, and the motive is mainly play. I meet very few serious commuters riding bicycles. I meet a great many ensconced in big cars, riding alone.

Yet think of the benefit if only fifty thousand Atlantic Canadians pedalled only five hundred miles a year to work; twenty-five million miles of car wear saved, and over one million gallons of gasoline that could be put to better use. Not to mention the health dividends. With oil prices rising and the Federal government running costly ads to improve national fitness, there never was a better time.

So go ahead. If you live within ten miles of work and your health is good, plan now to pedal to fitness and ecological redemption. Turn a deaf ear to tales about drunken drivers or rowdy dogs or even fleet bulls—but be careful. Ignore the Leacock buffs who fancy that the marvelous human body needs coddling.

Do your bit for clean air and lead-free daisies. Feel the wind again. Flex your muscles. Sweat a bit. Smell the roses and the pulp trucks. Tune in on the tree frogs. Taste the rain, swoop, glide, play hawk.

Of course you can expect the occasional put-down. My favourite was administered by a small boy. I had just wheeled up to Pike's Cycle Shop on Springdale Street in St. John's to buy a valve or something. As I dismounted I noticed him eyeing me narrowly.

"Hi," I said cheerfully. He kept glancing from me to my bike and frowning. After a few minutes he drew himself up.

"Are you a man?" he asked sternly.

"S-sure," I stammered.

A pregnant silence. Then he blurted out:

"*Mans* don't ride bikes!"

—*1976*

• A Wealth of Brooks •

It happens to me earlier some years. This year it was in February, during one of those sudden thaws. I can recall almost the precise moment. It was right after lunch one overcast Sunday afternoon. The air was so mild I went outside in shirtsleeves to inspect my half-acre estate. Somehow I felt curiously alert as I ambled about admiring the burlap-coloured fields patched with dirty snow, sniffing the tang of wet mud, kicking at old boards and rocks, forming a vague notion of doing something but not sure what.

Then, without warning, I got this powerful urge to wade a brook. Not to go fishing—though that's part of it; no, just to haul on a pair of long rubbers or old sneakers and spend a few hours splashing up and down a favourite brook.

Oh, I know it's childish. It's the sort of thing youngsters do in the spring, mucking around in trickles and puddles with their tin cans and sticks and toy boats, getting the feet soaking wet and their hands red and raw.

The beauty of it is, with a brook you can do the same thing while pretending you're trouting.

Of course, February is far too early in these parts. April or May is the time.

Most of us, if pressed, would admit to a favorite stream some- where in our past. Mine is eight hundred miles away, but no matter; it's easy to find a substitute. Atlantic Canada boasts plenty of them— all sizes; one thing we have is a wealth of brooks. My own choice is one that's too wide to jump but not so large that I run the risk of swamping my rubbers.

As I said, fishing makes this pastime respectable. So I always carry a soupcan full of fresh-dug garden worms and a bamboo pole. The pole comes in three parts and will fit in a small case. I don't bother with a reel. Reels are for fancy casting and proper playing of fish—things which good wading brooks don't lend themselves to. Normally there are too many overhanging branches and sunken logs.

One more bit of advice: don't take the kids along. Not on your first trip for the year, anyway. If that sounds sacreligious in this International Year of the Child, I can only plead that adults have rights, too. Is a few hours of solitary communion with nature after a hard winter too much to ask? I think not. Taking children fishing is vitally important. But do it later, when you're more up to untangling snarled lines and rescuing snagged hooks.

So here you are alone, let's say, heading for The Brook, feet snug and dry in wool socks, hip waders pulled high over warm pants, jacket pockets bulging with sandwiches and apples on one side and a can of worms on the other, fishing pole over your shoulder. The first wave of black flies is past. The mosquitoes and no-see-ums haven't got their bearings yet. The deer flies are two months away. Around you the landscape is as soft as a watercolour, all browns and grays. It's a late spring. The only greens are the sombre olive tones of spruce and fir, not yet brightened by new growth. The only reds are the crimson twigs of willows (now studded with satiny catkins), and a shrivelled rose hip here and there. Birch and alder are still leafless—though their brown catkins have stretched enough to give off puffs of sulfur pollen at the slightest touch.

And it's quiet. Except for the crunch of leaves underfoot, the occasional cawing of distant crows, or the reedy note of a chickadee close by, the woods have the deserted air of a dance floor the morning after a gala ball. Echoes and tokens of last summer's green and golden celebrations are everywhere: rich ferns matted in brown tangles, the hairy cup of a warbler's hidden nest now hung in plain view on a branch, last fall's polychrome carpet of leaves bleached as brown as leather.

The single animated feature is the brook. Through the sepia woods it comes, still faintly milky with meltwater, here running dark and foam-flecked under high banks, there dashing noisily across gravelly shallows, and, farther on, cascading in curtains of spray down shelves of wet shale.

Your first step into the icy water is both delectable and dangerous. Delectable, because the water presses in coolly on all sides against your legs. Dangerous, because one can never be sure one has found and patched all the leaks from the summer before. Even new rubbers sometimes have holes. So for a tense moment you wait, with one foot still on dry ground, for the first cold trickle. Let's say you're lucky. Or, at worst, that you brought along a small patching kit.

Now you can relax and *see* the brook. Gingerly you start walking. It's no ordinary kind of walking. It's more like putting one foot in front of the other. Each step is a small decision, a swift computation of mass, velocity, slope and slipperiness, calculated to keep you right side up. I know this sounds like work. On the contrary, it's the kind of primal thinking so seldom called for in our modern world of pavement and terrazo and indoor-outdoor carpeting that, paradoxically, it seems to clear the head. Don't rush things though. It takes a while for the overworked intellect to let go, to turn over the controls, to trust itself to the wisdom of the body. Until that occurs, walking a slimy uneven stream bed can be irritating. But when it does occur, you can actually feel the mind doing its spring cleaning. Out they go, all the rubbish of getting and spending, the sweepings of useless worries, the cobwebs and dust of discarded projects.

Still, it doesn't pay to daydream too deeply. Most brooks don't allow it for long. For as you come abreast of a sunken log the dark water is lit by a flash of bronze and a dark torpedo shape goes arrowing upstream—a trout!

In the excitement of brook-wading you almost forgot to fish. Moments later you're tempting this fellow with a worm. One, two, three tries...a strike! A brief tussle, during which you almost land on your backside in the stream, and you have him out on the bank, thumping his tail in the dry grass, a half-pounder if he's an ounce.

What colours they sport, those brookies: bellies milk-white, backs marbled in umber and black, sides all rosy-lavender like a summer dawn and freckled with scarlet and turquoise. It seems a shame to catch them. Until you remember the flavour....

Before the day is out you may have enough for a meal. If you're like me you'll wish again that you owned a proper creel, like the fishermen on the covers of *Outdoor Life* and *Field and Stream;* but you don't, because you're not really that serious an angler, so you make do (one more time) by threading your fish on a forked alder twig hung from your belt. Who knows? Maybe it improves the taste....

In such ways, like the brook itself, the day unfolds its simple surprises and delights. No need to dwell here on the startled grouse or deer that leaves you just as startled, the zigzag antics of water striders, the incredibly good taste of a plain lunch in the open air, the feeling of delicious exhaustion on the way home.

Think, now. Isn't there a brook somewhere that you owe a visit to for old time's sake?

"Sure," you retort, "but it's too polluted to be safe!"

In that case, may I suggest that you collect whatever support you need and clean it up.

Either way, don't wait for summer; do it now.

—1979

• River Talk •

The other day I happened to lunch with a Connecticut man. In the course of conversation we discovered that each of us had been born near a river. While this in itself wasn't noteworthy, the instant bond that sprang from this mere fact struck me as remarkable. Utter strangers moments before, here we were excitedly comparing notes like long-lost friends on the geography of his river and mine, on the fish that swam in them and the ducks that winged over them, on canoeing in summertime and skating in the winter. River talk, I call it. And I caught in his eye a look that I knew from of old, a faraway gaze that focused beyond the potted rubber plant and even beyond the lettered windows and their city skyline to rest somewhere over Connecticut.

The river I talked about was the Gander in northeast Newfoundland. My bond with it is many-stranded, coloured by mystery and magic and, above all, by stories heard in childhood. To grow up beside such a river and then leave it is somehow harder than leaving a hometown, I don't know why. Perhaps it is because a river seems to have a life of its own, forever flowing away yet forever there, in a way that a mountain or a street does not. And when four generations of one's ancestors have built their lives around it, as mine have done, family history becomes part of that life.

The Gander is about one hundred miles long and drains some five thousand square miles of the island between the Exploits watershed to the west and the Terra Nova watershed to the east. In pre-European times it was one of several waterways favoured by the Beothuk or Red Indian people for salmon fishing, caribou hunting and travelling between seacoast and interior. In the early 1700s,

English merchants began to land summer crews at its mouth to exploit the abundant salmon run. There were clashes with the Beothuk, who used guerrilla tactics to disrupt the fishery. In time gunpowder and tuberculosis won out. Settlers moved in from the exposed islands of Fogo and Twillingate to enjoy the abundance of timber and wild meat and furbearers.

When I came along in the 1930s, traces of this lifestyle still persisted. Uncle John Gillingham and Arthur and Alec Hodder and others still tended their salmon nets in season, loggers and trappers and guides still plied the river in homemade canoes, and the old people still remembered stories of the Beothuk. Some of those stories had already assumed the proportions of legends, but we children had no need for these; we could fabricate our own. Every sortie our fathers or uncles or older brothers made into 'The Country' yielded tales surpassing anything we heard on the radio (except perhaps *Superman*) or found in print (except perhaps *Tarzan*). The Country—a generic term covering roughly the Gander watershed—seemed to me at least as exotic and dangerous as the Amazon basin or the Valley of the Nile. And I could actually smell The Country on my father's homeknit sweater, a tantalizing blend of wood smoke and fir boughs and body odour. In furring season I caught a wild whiff of weasel, lynx or muskrat.

After each trip there always seemed to be a post-mortem at our house. Oldtimers who could no longer hunt or trap would drop in after teatime to hear my father recount his journeys and experiences. He was a good raconteur. Often I had to be chased to bed long before they quit. The stories were about caribou and moose, and accidents with gun or boat or fire, about a fine catch of fur, or how his sled dogs had led him back to camp through a blinding blizzard. Sometimes there were tales of the supernatural. Heady stuff for youngsters.

Although I cannot speak for the females among us then, we boys had no doubts whatever that, when we were big enough, we too would become rivermen. I know *I* intended to become one. The River was our highway, the central fact of our life. Oh, I might do a few other things, such as travel the world, become a monk, catch train robbers, paint masterpieces when I felt like it—but always in the background there would be my canoe, my dog team, my true vocation, my river.

It was not to be. In 1945, the year I was ten, my family left Gander Bay. It was to be the first of many peregrinations that took me farther and farther from the river. The reasons meant little to me

then. I know now that they had to do with such things as a job for my father, schooling for my brother and me, medical care and a few conveniences for my mother. In the Bay at that time we had neither running water nor electricity. My mother, never in robust health in those years, lived in dread of TB, diptheria and polio. Our nearest hospital was a full day's boat trip away—weather permitting. The winter trip was a nightmare until the bush plane broke our isolation.

The city was exciting to a ten-year-old. Miles of level sidewalks. Movie theatres and corner stores. And the motor cars—I remember the thrill of seeing my first street-full as I strolled with my parents to a movie at the Paramount Theatre in St. John's. To one who had seen no artificial light brighter than a flashlight beam, their headlights seemed like miniature suns. Compared to a motorboat or a canoe, their speed was a miracle. The warm breath of their exhaust seemed like the very incense of success. I still get a mild high from the smell of gasoline.

But our visits home became fewer. Eventually, in his forties, my father became fed up with city life and moved back for good to open a catering business. By then I was on the verge of manhood, with peregrinations of my own in mind. In the busy years that followed, years of intense study and exuberant learning, when the hours of day and night seemed too few for all there was to see and do, the reality of my river faded until it was a mere shadowy presence behind my thoughts, a moving silvery field of broken sunlight or moonlight, an image of coppery underwater grasses undulating like a woman's hair in the wind, a rainy whisper of wind in aspen leaves, a kingfisher's staccato cry among the birchy islands. Yet it was always there. Like Yeats' beloved waters of Innisfree, I heard them in the deep heart's core.

Whenever I could, I returned. On such occasions I rode in my father's or brother's or an uncle's canoe, not quite a tourist but not quite a native either, and stared at the landmarks and watermarks like Rolling Falls and Big Chute and Bread and Cheese Rock and the Sunshine Pool, and mused on my life. It seemed that somehow I had lost a century, slipped into another time. Only The River stayed the same. Between visits I began to write about and paint about my river and its rivermen. This helped. Later I scripted a television program and wrote a book. Perhaps when I am too old and gnarled to write or paint I shall build a hut and live beside my river and finally fathom the nature of its spell.

To stand on the bank of a river in the stillness of dawn or dusk and watch ponds and lakes of water glide by soundlessly in endless procession, ever changing yet ever the same, is like watching eternity spill through the mirror of time. To have spent a lifetime near such a river, however hard the life, has always seemed to me to be one of the luckier dispensations and therefore I admire and salute all real riverpeople—even those, who, like myself, merely have a certain faraway look in their eye.

—1986

• A Lawn for Scatari •

U ntil I visited Scatari Island that summer, the importance of lawn-keeping escaped me. I could never fathom why so many people treat their grassy plots as if their lives depended on them. The significance of the whole expensive ritual from bare soil to finished turf—all the rockpicking, raking, fertilizing, seeding, rolling, watering, reseeding, watering, refeeding, and then the summer routine of mowing and weeding until death do us part—was a mystery to me. To me it had all the logic of a dog chasing its tail.

Oh, I could see some good in lawns. They do look nice. Nobody likes getting soaked to the knees at his doorstep from rain or dew. Searching for lost toys or tools in waist-high grass is no fun. Being ambushed by garter snakes or toads can jolt some people. Ants and dandelions annoy others. Fires can start in tall dry grass and burn houses. And if we consider the lawn industry, I suppose they are even good for the economy.

But I still couldn't understand why thousands of North Americans, with the highways of a fantastically beautiful continent beckoning from their driveways, with so many exciting things to do, would opt for this unproductive servitude to a plot of grass. Bad enough to have to wash the car or walk the dog, I reasoned. Better to lay flagstone walks to keep one's shins dry, let the toys go missing, scythe a firebreak around the house, suffer the harmless wildlife and weeds, learn to landscape with hay, support the economy some other way, keep a goat, grow potatoes.

It was beyond me. Then I met this lighthouse keeper on Nova Scotia's bleak Scatari Island, where I went with some biologists to check on the well-being of some willow grouse imported from New-foundland as an experiment.

As our boat passed the island's rocky snouts snarling with white breakers that week in June, lawns were the furthest thing from my mind. Admiring the stunted fir thickets blasted by salty gales, the dun and ochre boglands ribbed with worn granite and laced with black ponds, I couldn't have imagined a patch of Kentucky blue or fescue there if I'd tried. Listening to the reptilian blasts of the fog horn or the mewing of gulls in the mists, who could have guessed that a lawnmower sang here on fine summer mornings? It offended one's concept of wilderness. It was unthinkable.

But it was true. The keeper of the light also kept a lawn. Proudly he showed it to us, a small square of green, suffering from exposure, but obviously not from lack of love. He showed us his mower, too. Gleaming in green and gold, it was truly a magnificent machine, complete with clipping bag and finger controls. The Department of Transport had supplied it on his request, he explained. They were good that way, he added.

At the moment, unfortunately, the mower outshone the lawn. He had only started growing it the year before. He allowed there were certain problems in such an exposed location. But he wasn't daunted. He spoke lovingly of his plans for it, how he would fertilize here and reseed there. He expounded the ecological intricacies of lawn-tending, amazed me with the botanical secrets of *Gramineae*. For the bald spots he proposed to seek out and transplant hardy native grasses from elsewhere on the island. Already he could picture his sward lush and ankle-deep, bending before the powerful mower. As he talked his eyes had the look gardeners get when the new seed catalogues arrive in January.

I was shocked and sobered. Here was a man whose job I envied, ensconced on a wild and lovely island I already loved, who hankered for the ordered ranks of suburbia. Or did he? He must love the island too; how else could he live here? Then why this seeming conformity?

Suddenly I saw how deep this lawn thing goes with us. I saw that it was not a rationale at all, but an absurdity—like so many other things in life. Like dancing or socializing or hunting, it seemed to be rooted in a primal human urge. Maybe it even went back to the beginnings of agriculture, or beyond that to the nomadic parkland existence of our hominid ancestors, for whom, say the anthro-pologists, sunny open grassland meant freedom from the jungle's terrors. Far from being just a vacuous itch to keep up with the

Joneses, perhaps lawnkeeping partook of the ancient magic of seeds, of our deep need to impose some modicum of order on the fearsome excesses of nature. How else explain this lawn on rugged Scatari?

Far-fetched as my explanation seemed, it helped me.

A few days later, our work with the ptarmigan done, we left the Island. As the lighthouse with its green patch receded behind our wake, I thought of the lightkeeper, pipe in mouth, mowing his lawn like everyone else on a summer's morning.

The sound of his machine might be drowned in the booming of Atlantic combers at his doorstep; no matter. Before it reached his nostrils the fragrance of fresh-cut grass would be swept away by sea-winds; no matter. Instead of crabgrass and dandelions he would contend with guano and sea urchins dropped by wheeling gulls; no odds. In place of a pretty barberry hedge with butterflies, a hollyhocked white picket fence for border, his lawn would abut a lighthouse wall and slope down to swaying rockweed and jagged rocks studded with blue mussels and pink barnacles. On warm August evenings, when suburbanites in Charlottetown or Fredericton sat on patios sipping cool drinks and conversing, he could climb the winding stair and admire his sward as the great light swept across it and out to sea. When crazy winter storms tore at his walls and freezing spray blurred his windows and visions of dying ships haunted him, he could take comfort in the thought of his grass sleeping under the snow to brighten another spring. Not a poet of words, he could be a poet of grass. Keeper of a light, he would also keep a lawn.

—1975

• Walkabout •

Once a year, after the heat of summer but before the snow flies, I like to give myself a small vacation, a solitary excursion by motor car with no particular itinerary save enjoying the land and the people, taking a long look at a tree or a headland, listening to the crows bark and the apples drop, smelling the sharp tea fragrance of fallen leaves and the musk of distant skunk, saying hello to myself again. If you will, a walkabout, as the Australians call it. We all need one now and then.

Two years ago on Labour Day weekend I drove to Nova Scotia's Parrsboro Shore on such an excursion. My excuse was landscape painting. This Glooscap country is rich not only in legends. It offers stern headlands and secret coves, satiny mudflats, plunging streams, tawny fields and rolling hardwood hills.

People here log, fish and farm for a living. On the side they bring in a few extra dollars from tourism—like the Rockhound Festival in August—and from blueberries and maple syrup. The feeling is a bit like Cape Breton.

My jaunt took me from Truro to Advocate and back. I painted only four panels. Yet I cherish some images that I know will outlast my memories of Mississauga and the 401 at rush hour.

Painting outdoors has one great advantage. It allows one to sit and stare at something for three or four hours without risking impoundment for insanity. Saturday dawned sunny. I drove north from Parrsboro, where I had stayed overnight in a rented cottage, up toward Halfway River. The blueberry fields were just turning wine and gold and I wanted to do something with them. The sawdust pile of an abandoned sawmill provided the vantage point I needed. All afternoon, while I painted a hillside farm and fields reflected in a cobalt blue lake, two loons sported and called to each other in the waters below.

My first study of the trip completed, I drove back through town and out to Parrsboro Beach to eat supper and spend the night. The beach is spectacular and I wanted to be ready to paint there early the next morning. It is two beaches really, a short one facing east, a longer one facing west, and both curving south to meet the high wooded hump known as Partridge Island. Between them, sheltered from the fierce Fundy tides by the two ridges of sand and cobble, is a triangle of green saltmarsh where ducks come and breezes play delicate games. Fair across Minas Basin, about five miles away, looms Cape Blomidon with the snaggled teeth of Cape Split off to the right.

Before turning in for the night I decided to walk out around the island far enough to see not just the western half of Blomidon, but all of it. This would mean walking perhaps a quarter mile—but since the tide had just fallen there was no need to scramble along the cliffs. In fact, the tide had fallen much farther than usual because it was the time of the full moon, and a neap tide at that. As I slid and stumbled over the wet kelp and slimy rocks I marvelled at just how far it had gone out. Down to the water's edge looked like a long walk. Everything was still dripping wet, still draining in rivulets toward the Basin, toward the setting sun that turned everything crimson.

I still couldn't see all of Blomidon. To my left rose two-hundred-foot turrets and towers of eroded basalt topped by wind-torn spruce. They, too, looked rosy in the sunset, but I was trying to imagine climbing those cliffs should the sea decide to return. My logical mind said: "Wait, the tide doesn't start to rise again for three hours yet...." But my imagination and my body suddenly wanted out of there.

A dozen yards more. And there, spread out along the southern horizon like a huge battleship camouflaged in pink and mauve, sat all ten miles of Blomidon, legendary home of Glooscap. It *was* majestic. But I didn't linger. As I climbed the interminable slippery slope back to the high and dry I thought of an ant labouring up the sides of a child's sandbox.

It felt good to be in the station wagon. Parked as it was in the lee of the island's wooded northern slope, it made a tolerably good camp. Tilting the reclining seat down all the way and wriggling into my sleeping bag, I tuned the radio to CBC and lay back to enjoy the night. As the full September moon lifted over the Cobequid Hills far down the basin, I heard the urbane voice of Arthur Lowey unfolding from his imaginary train "The Continental Express" the beauties of the music of the Spanish bullring. The last I heard was a fanfare of trumpets. Hours later I saw, or dreamed I saw, the bay brimming with quicksilver. Had I died and gone to heaven?

Hot, blinding sunlight and the roar of a mosquito in my ear jolted me back to reality. Stiff and hungry, I climbed from the car. The high tide had come within a dozen yards of my wheels, and the cobbles were just drying off. I made a sketch of the moon, pale now and ghostly as it set over nearby Cape Sharp.

While I ate breakfast a white Lada came down the far hill, crept out across the beach and parked. Two old gentlemen in Sunday suits and hats climbed out on one side. The driver, a middle-aged man in a white turtleneck, got out on the other. For a while they stood surveying the morning. Then they moseyed over to see what I was up to. We greeted one another with the cordiality people feel on a sparkling morning by the sea. They commented kindly on my picture. A while later we went our separate ways.

Halfway to Advocate, somewhere around Brookville, I stopped once more to paint. Back toward Truro the basin was awash with pastel shades of blue and pink and green, and in the autumn haze Cape Sharp and Partridge Island and Economy Head stood one behind the other like mountains in a Chinese landscape. I climbed

the guard rail and found a comfortable spot down the slope under a telephone line in the warm sun. Far below me was a tiny red-roofed house and a barn, and to my left the narrow ribbon of road looped over the evergreen hills. For several hours I lost track of time as I looked and daubed, looked and daubed. A cricket chirred. A warbler sang. It was one of those perfect autumn afternoons made of sunshine and stillness.

Afterward, cleaning up, I heard a squeal of brakes and a car door slam. A lanky fellow jumped out, crossed the road and stood staring at the bay. Around his neck was an expensive camera and other accoutrements.

He wasn't looking my way, so I went back to rinsing my brushes. Next thing I heard was: "Dammit, they've gone and put the telephone poles in the way." The photographer then slammed his door on the Chinese mountains, spun gravel over the goldenrod, and was gone.

Advocate Harbour, spread out like a neat toy village behind its barachois, deserved at least a week. I had only a few hours. Already the sun was low again. I painted it turning the windowpanes to liquid gold. I sketched an apple tree. Then I had to stow my gear for good and start the two-and-one-half-hour drive back. It was a long, looping, roller-coaster trip, chasing my lengthening shadow along the pavement. But this time I was content just to look, and felt no desire to stop. Again the moon rose—not quite so round this time—and again it silvered the waters. Happily I followed it home.

—1984

• A Pleasure of Place Names •

W hat a way they had with place names, our forebears. If you or I had to name a place we'd have to consult professors and lawyers, and even then we'd come up with one of those insipid Mapletons or Glendales, as like as not.

Yet it seems our unlettered ancestors knew no such qualms. No sooner had they clapped eyes on a new headland or bay or hill than they had a perfect name for it. And the names still keep their flavour and colour. How to account for this knack? How is it that we with all our advantages can't seem to manage a decent name for a weekend cottage? How can Breakheart Point and Dunromin both issue from the same mother tongue?

Maybe it has to do with depth of involvement in the landscape. Our grandparents didn't just visit it on weekends; they lived and died in its embrace. Naming the features of their native geography must have been as natural for them as nicknaming friends is for us.

All this was brought home to me when I was confronted with an unusually large map of Newfoundland. When it comes to twenty-four-carat place names, surely no other piece of North American real estate is so richly endowed. This particular map was so big that it had names seldom seen on smaller charts. In no time I was searching out hidden nuggets. Ignoring such shopworn examples as Come by Chance and Heart's Content, I began to work my way up the west coast from Cape Ray.

This coast is thinly settled, but I found places like Little Friar's Cove, Tweed Island, Cow Head, Parson's Pond, River of Ponds, Spirity Point, Dog Pen, Garagamelle. And Harbour Harbour. After Nameless Cove I swung round the northern tip, between Belle Isle (with its Black Joke Cove) and Great Sacred Island, and made south along the east side of the peninsula. Past Hare Bay with Great Cormorandier Island at its mouth I went, past Conche and the Grey Islands, until I came to Englee in Canada Bay. Here I paused to recall a few weeks I'd spent there, and the old boat builder who taught me how to tell whether a new spar was sound.

"You hangs a pocket watch on one end like this," he explained, "and if you can't hear the ticking at the other end there's bad wood in her."

I continued southward where places like Great Harbour Deep (Orange Bay on old sea charts) and Great Cat Arm perch in their tarns and still rely on the CN coastal boat for outside goods. Crossing White Bay from Devil Point to Fleur de Lys, I coasted past Grappling Point and Confusion Bay, rounded Manful Head and came to the dense geography of Notre Dame Bay, my native waters.

I dawdled among its filigreed headlands and islands, savouring such delights as Virgin Arm, Leading Tickles West and Comfort Cove. I looked in at Whale's Gulch, Bumblebee Bight, Coal All Island, Salt Pans and Seldom-Come-By; did a turn around Fogo-Twillingate-Moreton's Harbour (of *I'se the B'y That Builds the Boat* fame); and then set off on an easterly tack that brought me in between Doting Cove and Offer (outer) Wadham Island, to make port at last between the twin Bills of Cape Freels.

In Bonavista Bay there are two Wolf Islands—our grandfathers feared this animal most of all. But there are no wolves here any more to frighten their children in their beds. And Mouse Island; also an animal to reckon with. They were thought to have truck with witches and in some years were known to swarm, devouring all in their path and sometimes bringing famine in their wake. Parts of Nova Scotia suffered such a plague in the 1800s, and even now certain offshore islands without cats or foxes swarm with mice some summers.

Of all the island names, I liked the descriptive ones best—Tumbler Island, for instance, or Bakers Loaf Island. Likewise with Ship, Pincher (as in pliers), Pouch and Mustard Bowl.

Most of all, I liked not their quaintness but their audacity. To name a baby—flesh of our flesh—is one thing. But to take a feature of the landscape, a thing that may have existed for eons before one was born, and casually give it a label is surely something else. Especially when that feature is some forbidding piece of geography like, say, a dangerous headland that has been known to kill ships and drown sailors. For the survivors of those disasters to turn around and tag such a thing with a name like 'Jerry's Nose' is a fine and human gesture indeed. Even a kind of literature.

—1977

SAUNDERS

Homecomings

...I am not sure how much I speak with the voice of that time or how much in the voice of what I have since become.

Alistair MacLeod
As Birds Bring Forth the Sun

• Homecomings •

When I went home to Gander Bay that spring, my father and I travelled down the river in his canoe, as always. The thirty-mile trip to the Bay took about two hours. The year was 1956, yet unless you hired a float plane or hiked through the woods, the Gander River was still the only way to get from Glenwood on the rail line to our village on the northeast coast.

There never will be a better way. Or so it seemed to me, a book-weary college student coming home to visit between winter studies and summer work, drinking in the sights and sounds and smells again as only homesick youth can.

For The River was our road. More than that, it was a Presence. Joseph Conrad remarked that sailors always referred to the Cape of Good Hope as *The* Cape. In the same spirit Gander Bay people always said *The* River. Not that it is notable as rivers go. Atlases seldom mention it. The salmon fishing is famous, but there are no scenic wonders and no great battles were fought nearby. And not that it is very dangerous, except sometimes in spring. Though they have taken a few lives, its white waters are not fierce enough to rate the Wild Rivers catalogue.

Yet as children we thought the Gander at least as mighty as the Nile or Amazon we read about in school, and in our minds its headwaters rose somewhere near the roof of the world. We didn't know then that it is merely an ancient and shallow stream of the braided sort, a scant hundred miles from source to sea.

No matter. To take a canoe and navigate The River as deftly as our fathers was every boy's ambition in Gander Bay. For in such a shallow and braided river the runs were hard to learn. They formed a downhill labyrinth of rapids, islands and channels strewn with gray boulders, and the channels changed with every cloudburst and season. Some men never mastered them. Their navigational errors were chalked up in coloured paint on the submerged rocks—or worse could happen. Other men, reading the telltale eddies with eyes asquint, could unravel the intricate water skeins with hardly a bump, by starlight if need be. They were our boyhood heroes.

To our elders this river was also a livelihood; a good catch of otter or lynx, a caribou for the winter hunger, the silver lunge of salmon for a well-cast Blue Charm to please the wealthy sport from Baltimore or Toronto, a good pile of paper birch to feed the kitchen stove to make the tea to help them face another day.

One might say The River cast a spell. From childhood to adulthood some never shook the magic, or wished to. And all the traffic was by canoe in summer and by dog team in winter.

Ten years later when I went home, my father and I motored along a new gravel highway. It was a pretty good road, too, running more or less with The River, cutting a clean swath through dark spruce hollows and bright birch glades, not breaking stride for shale cliffs or small brooks, wasting no miles on meandering.

Now and then from the speeding car I would glimpse the Gander a mile or two away among the hills. It looked strange. With shock I realized that from this angle it looked *ordinary*. The way a stranger might see it....

This time it took us only forty minutes to reach the familiar landscape of the Bay. Everything looked smaller than I remembered. Yet The River, diminished as it was by this new road, reasserted its sovereignty at the estuary, where the people lived. Home for us was on the far shore. There was no bridge yet. Boatmen ourselves, we had to hire one to ferry us across.

At dusk, returning from a visit to my aged grandmother, I could see against the twilight sky upstream a causeway taking shape. Tall power pylons marched down to the water. They seemed artificial, like props for a play. Ahead, as we neared the darkening shore, supper lights gleamed across the water. They looked somehow different than I remembered; brighter, steadier, harder. Then I recalled seeing linemen stringing wires on new poles that day. We were witnessing the advent of electricity to this side of the Bay. Long-awaited like the road, 'the power' had finally come.

Suddenly there flashed across my mind three images of isolation. My brother tossing in pain with severed fingers for two interminable days and nights of howling blizzard, awaiting the bush plane to take him to a doctor. Sick women enduring rough voyages over wintry seas to the nearest hospital twenty-five miles away on Twillingate Island. Our school locked and barred all winter for lack of teachers willing to brave the isolation.

Now such spectres would fade. Good riddance.

Yet even while rejoicing in these gains, I felt a twinge of betrayal that the strong brown river god of our childhood was being thus diminished by the very sort of knowledge our generation had left home to seek. Instead of learning to be rivermen like our fathers, reading litanies of rock and ripple, calligraphies of water and granite, we were becoming technicians of concrete and kilowatts.

On my next visit we needed no ferryman or canoe. Causeway and bridge were now complete. From the bridge, kids with strangely familiar faces dangled fishing poles and exchanged news of *Bugs Bunny* and *Spiderman*. The River was no longer a road or a presence, and boys would no longer study to be its votaries. Far upstream, hydroelectric impoundments were already drowning the old campsites and trapping grounds.

This time I was driving my own car, with my young family aboard. Before I knew it we were across The River and halfway through the village. The smallness of everything astonished me anew. The Bay seemed shrunk to insignificance. A new highway had swallowed familiar fences and gardens and now threatened the very doorsteps of the cowering houses. The former road, a footpath by comparison, where strolling lovers had heard sheep and goats bleat sleepily under the moon, had vanished without trace.

At fifty miles an hour one could bound over my River and tear through my village without knowing that a presence or a place were there at all. For lack of a plan, for lack of a desire to sift the old and good from the merely old, they were vanishing down the road to progress.

—1975

• Airplanes of my Childhood •

A bject terror pretty well describes my reaction to the first airplane I ever saw up close. It's a wonder I didn't hate planes for
the rest of my life. Yet today I regard them with affection, especially
bush planes.

It happened one gray afternoon the summer I was ten. I was
fishing eels alone on the old government wharf when I heard this
low thundery rumble from the north. There was nothing to be seen
in that direction except Sandy Cove Island and some clouds, but the
sound soon took on the wind-baffled drone of an airplane. Then I
saw it, a huge gray whale of a thing, its stepped belly slung low under
a high straight wing on which two big engines were perched.
Skimming the calm water it came in so low I thought it might land.
Because the plane was still downwind, the voice of its motors
seemed too small for its bulk. But now the sound grew, peeling off
layer after layer until I dropped my fishing pole, clapped hands over
ears and dived for cover in the wharf. Hiding among the rotting
timbers, fervently repenting sins past and present (especially that of
venturing onto the forbidden wharf alone), I saw the sky swiftly
darken and felt the pilings quiver and the very ballast rocks quake
under my knees.

Then my eardrums were assaulted by the loudest, most violent
noise I'd ever heard, louder than my uncle's sawmill in full career,
louder than the spring ice leaving Clarke's Brook, louder even than
midnight muskets on New Year's Eve. Had it lasted more than a few
seconds I could not have stood it; but suddenly the sky brightened
and the sound was dying down and when I peeked out between the

pilings the monster was already fading against the dark hills to the south and I was safe.

When I told my father about it that night (without mentioning the wharf), he just smiled. "Oh," he said, "that was just an old *Catalina Flying Boat*. Scared you, did it?" I nodded. "That's one big ugly plane, for sure. The pilot was probably doing a practice run."

Just knowing the monster's name made me feel better.

During the war, living as we did between the new airport at Gander and the seaplane base at Botwood, we children got to know quite a few aircraft by sight and sound. But except for a *Hurricane* fighter that crashed and was brought out the river in three pieces, I had never seen one up close.

The war plane we saw most often and liked best was the *Harvard Trainer*, a butter-yellow, single-engine fighter with a two-man cockpit, blunt nose and stubby wings. Sometimes they swooped so low over the meadows and potato gardens—terrorizing the sheep and goats and horses—that we could actually see the goggled faces of the men who flew them. Because they never landed, we never met the pilots. Like Pizarro's horsemen they remained mythic creatures, part man, part Other. And we, like wonder-struck Incas, worshipped them. We even made images of their steeds; wooden models in summer, snow replicas in winter. In fact, on mild days when the snow was just right it was common to see a squadron of us at recess time, darting and diving our hand-held fighters in loud and earnest dogfights around the school grounds.

The planes and fliers we knew best were the ones who came after the war to ferry mail and passengers, the workhorse bushplanes and their legendary pilots. In wintertime they would land on the ice and taxi in near shore. We could walk right up to them. Sheer magic, this—to know a thing in both its near and far aspects, to know an aeroplane both as a shining mote against the sun, unreachable and godlike, and in its cabled and rivetted reality, touchable in skis and struts and paint-scuffed wings. My heart would pound with excitement as, standing with the inevitable knot of sky-gazers, I watched the coming aircraft slide down and down, now dark against the turquoise sky, now bright against the purple hills, now bouncing its skis against the faraway ice in one, two, three spurts of snow; now turning to charge across the Bay toward us, chased by its own small blizzard, to come to rest only yards away, its propellor materializing ghostlike from one silvery disk to two solid blades that chop-chopped the air more and more slowly until they halted in a final kickback, followed by a loud silence. And then to see the leather-jacketed pilot, a real human being after all with legs and arms like ours, climb stiffly down, turn to face us, and smile.

And later to experience those sensations in reverse—except that when the plane turns the blizzard engulfs you, stinging your eyes and cheeks with fine, gasoline-scented ice crystals so that you knuckle your eyes to clear them, not wishing to miss the always startling moment of lift-off nor the swift shrinking of an even tinier pilot within.

Strange as these metamorphoses seemed, it was stranger yet to witness one of those sky machines lying landbound and crippled.

The first accident I recall involved a *Fox Moth*, a single-engine wood-and-canvas biplane. What errand brought it I forget; but when the pilot came back after lunch and went to give the prop a crank or two by hand to choke the engine before switching on the ignition, it coughed and came to life.

Had someone tampered with the controls? Or had he himself forgotten and left the switch on? In seconds the wooden prop was a gleaming blur. He came near losing his arm. The throttle was set so high that the plane immediately began to move forward, at first slowly, then with mounting speed. Vainly the pilot tried to open the door and climb in. The crowd fell back in disbelief. They saw him lose his footing and fall, get up, run alongside, try again. He could catch up to it, but the twin wings and multiple struts hampered his climbing aboard. Ahead lay open ice—with my grandfather fair in the plane's path. Grandpa, realizing he was in a game of tag, tried to escape. In his youth he had been a speed skater. But now he was stout and slow. It was no use to run. As the plane overtook him he dropped flat on the ice. Its bottom wing barely cleared his ample form.

And now the runaway aircraft, its motor roaring, was approaching liftoff speed and fairly bouncing over the ice. At the same time it was swinging in a wide arc. To their horror the onlookers saw it turn back toward them. It seemed to have a mind of its own. Not knowing which way to run, they scattered like frightened hens. Moments later there was a splintering crash, then silence. The plane had collided with a rock-filled pier. No one was hurt.

Fixing the *Moth* took more than a month. Another plane brought canvas and wood and glue and a new propellor. My grandfather's vacant storehouse became the hangar. Every day after school I'd come to watch. I can still smell the acetone-banana oil odours of the dope and glue they used in mending the balsa skeleton and the torn canvas. Toward the end I suffered mixed emotions; I was sorry to see the job finished, but happy to see the *Fox Moth* fly again.

Another mishap involved a much larger aircraft, the all-metal *Norseman*. The *Norseman* came to pick up a sick woman on the north side of the Bay at Clarke's Head, our village. The pilot, Group Captain David Anderson, had been given a map which led him to think she lived on the south side. Discovering this too late, he was taxiing across the mile-wide expanse to our side. Now the Bay here is actually the estuary of the Gander, a river big enough to wear the ice thin, except in the coldest weather, for a mile down the middle of the Bay. This channel is the last to freeze in the fall and the first to open in the spring. Wisely, the pilot kept the engine revved to near takeoff speed as he headed across. However, he still didn't know exactly where the patient lived, and when he spotted a man walking across, he swung toward him to ask directions.

It was a mistake. The instant the *Norseman* slowed down and its full weight settled onto the ice the skis broke through. While the walking man watched helplessly, the tail section reared and the plane did a slow nose-dive right up to its wings—which kept it from going to the bottom. The pilot and his engineer, hearing the motor hissing and seeing the propellor churning the icy water to a froth and the water gurgling up around their legs, wrenched open the overhead emergency hatch and scrambled out across the wing to safety.

As for the sick woman, someone wired Gander for another plane, which came and took her that day.

The next few weeks were fascinating for me. After all attempts to prise the plane up and out with long poles failed, my father thought he saw a way to do it. During the war it was he who had salvaged the downed *Hurricane* fighter, bringing it fifteen miles downriver in sections on two canoes lashed together catamaran-style.

By comparison this was fairly simple. First he let the open water around the aircraft freeze solid. When the ice was strong enough he sunk poles in the bottom and erected a timber scaffold directly above the aircraft. From this he slung a double-sheave chain block and fastened hooks to the four lifting rings on top of the fuselage. With everything ready he chopped a hole around the plane large enough to permit the skis and front end to be hoisted through. Heavy planks were next slid into position, ready to be placed across the hole under the skis once the airplane cleared the water.

Whether the men sang 'Johnny Poker' as they hove on the straining rope, or some other rousing boathauling shanty from seventeenth century Devonshire, I don't recall. They likely did. It was the custom. In any case the drowned *Norseman* began to inch skyward.

Moments later, while the tripod creaked and water streamed from the ice-crusted cylinders and cockpit, the front half emerged into the light of day. When the skis were high enough someone shoved the planks across. The plane was rotated into position and gently lowered. Then it was just a matter of letting the hole freeze over again.

Before any repairs could be done the engine had to be thawed out. Heavy tarpaulins were draped over the front half of the plane and a gas heater was kept going day and night until everything was dry. Next there came a mechanic in a lovely little green and gold *Piper Cub*. Thanks to the river's dilution of the salt water, he found little serious damage. By replacing the electrical system and cleaning and oiling pistons and valves and such, they soon had it back in the air. Not long afterward the same plane was flown to Montreal for a new engine. The pilot, Joe Gilmore of Gander, met a snowstorm and crashed to his death somewhere on Prince Edward Island.

As a youngster I never craved a model plane. Perhaps it was because I enjoyed so much of the real thing: the magnificent lumbering *Consolidated Catalina*, the brash *North American Harvard*, the frail and ghostly DeHaviland *Fox Moth*, the muscular *Norseman*, the deadly Hawker *Hurricane*, the pretty *Piper Cub*. And because I could spin out my fantasies by drawing them. This I did, over and over. The one I drew best was the *Harvard*. You coloured it with your brightest yellow crayon—not forgetting the black patch in front of the cockpit, which was long and high with eight arches.

The other day, quite by accident, in a book called *The Tools of War*, I came across a photograph of the *Harvard*. It looked exactly as I remembered. Excitedly I read the vital statistics:

> ...two seat advanced trainer, better known as the Yellow Peril... 6000 horsepower, fully aerobatic...all-metal stressed-skin construction. Maximum speed 205 mph at 5,000 feet....

It sent the old tingle up my spine.

—1979

• Sawmill Song •

Noise pollution!
That's what I'd call it now. But when I was eight I thought that being wakened by a sawmill six days a week was part of summertime.

The first sound came at 6:30 a.m. when they rang the bell. Its clear high-pitched peal would wake anyone who wasn't a heavy sleeper. If that didn't, the engine would. First it would wheeze and cough. That was when my uncle, having primed it and slipped off the belt that drove the main shaft, was cranking the big flywheel. When the engine caught, the noise was like a salvo of shotgun blasts that came faster and louder until you thought the engine would tear itself apart.

But when he put the belt back onto the pulley, the effect was like saddling a lively horse. In a minute the bangs died down and the whole mill began to rumble and come to life. Gradually the engine would hit its stride again, until the first log hit the headsaw. Then the sawmill commenced to sing its true song. After that nobody could sleep; least of all me.

Without someone big to hold our hand we were never allowed in my uncle's sawmill while it was going. "You might stick your finger in a saw," they said, wagging their heads and frowning, "or catch your clothes in the belts." Then would follow warning tales about the man who was nearly killed by a flying slab or the man who absent-mindedly reached past a saw for something and drew back his hand minus three fingers.

But sometimes after supper, when the mill was shut down for the night and everything was still except for the sheep and goats bleating and bumping around underneath, we used to sneak in. At first we couldn't see anything. When our eyes got used to the dim light we saw that the ground was covered with sawdust and bits of rind that fell through the cracks in the floor above, which was why the walking was so soft.

At first it smelled like the woods. After a while you noticed grease and gasoline odours too. These came mostly from the engine.

The engine was black as a bear and twice as big, with a wheel on either side as high as a man and a square tank on top where steam came out when the engine was going fast. That was to keep it cool, they said. If someone lifted you up by the legs when the engine was going you could look down in the tank and see the black water wrinkling; but the noise up close like that was so loud you would get afraid and start to bawl and they would have to take you outside.

You couldn't run or play tag under the mill because it was full of posts and pulleys and shafts and belts. The posts were as big as trees and held up the whole mill. Some of them had whiskers of white wool on their corners where sheep had squeezed by, looking for a place to sleep or to get out of the rain or to chew their cuds.

The pulleys were shaped something like a Life-Saver and were turned by a steel shaft as thick as a man's arm. Some pulleys were the size of a cook pot and others the size of a big washtub. They were made of little pieces of wood all fitted together so you could hardly make out the seams, and when you ran your hand over the round part it felt as cool and smooth as glass from wearing against the belt.

Each belt ran on two pulleys like a clothesline. The belts were made of hard black rubbery canvas as thick as a pencil, and they too were worn shiny. They were not made in one piece but were laced or zippered together in sections. The wider a pulley and belt, the more power it had to carry. The widest was a foot across and it ran off the steel pulley on the engine. When a bigger pulley turned a smaller one the smaller one went faster, and when a smaller one turned a bigger one the bigger one went slower. Most of the belts ran level, but a few slanted up through holes in the floor above, where they turned the saws and ran the carriage.

Up in the mill it smelled less of gasoline and more of the woods, especially at the end facing the Bay, where the logs came up from the boom. The boom was a floating train of long, peeled poles chained together through holes bored at each end. It kept the logs from driving away when they were being towed down the Bay, and from leaving the Cove while waiting to be sawn. Even so, if there was a big storm the boom sometimes broke and the logs got out and drove ashore everywhere and had to be rounded up in boats and towed back, a slow job. And some of them went out the Bay and were lost for good.

The slip where the logs came up from the water had a chain up the middle with sharp iron points on it called dogs. The chain moved about as fast as a man walking slow. They called it the green chain because it hauled the wet logs up into the mill. A man worked at the foot of the slip all day long, nudging the logs toward the chain with a long pole they called a pick pole. Now and then he would row out in a dory to round up more logs. Sometimes he would let you in the boat with him—though he wasn't really supposed to.

When each log reached the top of the slip it would tip up and you could see water dripping from it as it inched out of sight. But if you climbed up and looked inside you would see it waiting its turn like a big, scaly, wet, brown fish alongside several others, while nearby a low table on iron wheels rushed back and forth on railway track, carrying a log that was being sawed. That was the carriage. A man with a peavey rolled each log on and clamped it tight. Going through the headsaw the carriage went slowly, especially when it carried a big log. But on the way back, with nothing to slow it down, it charged like a ram—and stopped just as suddenly. Then the sawyer would roll the log over so he could take a slab or board off the other side. Each time the carriage went forward the big shiny saw sang in the wood and a slab or a yellow board would flop over onto the rollers; and each time the carriage rushed back the sawyer, working his levers, would unclamp the log, flip it, clamp it again, and send it back.

The sawyer was the most important man in a mill, my father said, because he decided how many and what size boards would come out of each log. He did this all by eye, in seconds, standing with a gloved hand on the levers, his clothes and eyebrows grey with wood dust. To keep splinters and sawdust from flying in his face there was a burlap bag hung between him and the headsaw.

When the whole log had been sawn into planks and slabs, the man with the peavey would roll the next log onto the carriage and clamp it. This went on all day long, except when they shut down the mill for lunch or to file a saw or to fix something.

The planks still had bark on two sides, so after they left the headsaw they travelled down a slight hill on wooden rollers to the edgerman, who used a smaller saw to take a thin strip off each edge.

Then, at the far end of the mill, the trimmerman pulled a still smaller saw across each board to make it the right length.

At last the finished boards came out into the daylight and slid down some more rollers to where a man put them on his back and carried them to a trolley. When he had a load he would push the trolley along a set of tracks to the lumber yard, where he sorted them by length and width and thickness and stacked them neatly on high piles to dry. Sometimes after supper we rode on the trolley. But we had to be careful not to put our feet under the wheels. We never played much in the yard. The ground was nice and soft because it was built of years and years of sawdust and bark; but unless the day was cloudy or breezy, it was too hot in there among all the tall stacks of lumber, and so bright on sunshiny days that you could hardly keep your eyes open.

If you didn't keep your eyes open, though, you might get stung by a Timber Fly. Timber Flies were as long as your finger with white stripes all over their shiny black bodies, even on their legs and feelers. They couldn't fly very fast on their rattly wings, but they moved their legs in angry jerks as they walked over the lumber, and their feelers were always quivering as if they were mad at you. The worst thing was their black Stinger. It was an inch long and would—we believed—kill you right quick if they stuck it in you. (None of us suspected that this 'stinger' was used for laying eggs in wood.)

I think the nicest thing about the lumber yard was the smell of the fresh spruce and fir wood after it rained.

Besides lumber there was always nogs and slabs and edgings and sawdust coming from the mill. Nogs were the short ends made by the trimmerman. Most of the slabs were long and skinny; too floppy for a fishing pole but all right for kindling. Most of this was burned in a pile on the beach when the wind was in easterly and wet.

Sawdust disposal was a bigger problem. After several years there was no place left to put it. People used some for making ice-houses; but that didn't take much. Once the land around the mill was full to the water's edge they began to haul it back to the alder swamp. First they made a road of sawdust over the wet meadow where the blue-flag irises grew. Cart-load by cart-load it nosed along, in past Farrell's place, in past the horse-barn, then spreading out year after year until the whole swamp was one blond prairie of sawdust.

Most of that sawdust was hauled by one small horse, King, driven by an old man called Silas. Silas smoked a crooked pipe and was very gentle. Because the wheel rims made no noise at all in the sawdust, the only sounds the cart made were the thumps and squeaks like sometimes just before you fall asleep. We used to ride with old Silas now and then. He was fun to talk to; but King was so slow that soon we went looking for something else to do.

Even at the far end of the Sawdust Road you could still hear the mill. In fact, if the wind was right you could hear it from a mile or two in the woods, where we sometimes went trouting with the bigger boys. The rest of the time, whether we were jigging sculpins off the wharf of trapping sticklebacks in tidal pools or teasing the billy goat or playing boats in the cove or hunting fool's gold along the beach or prising spruce gum off beached logs or swimming at Point Head, the sawmill made our background music all summer. When it was shut down for repairs, and when it closed down for the winter, the world seemed strangely quiet.

The nicest mill sounds came after supper when the sawfiler did his work. Tooth by tooth he would go, stroking high notes from the small saws and low notes from the large. As the sun wheeled down the sky, its salmon-pink rays would reach at last into and under the mill, splashing the posts and beams with stripes of purple and gold. Robed in this light, the old man would work until the sky turned from gold to green to indigo; then he would clump down the steps and trudge home in the cool twilight, leaving the sleepy sheep to complain for a time in their sawdusty beds.

—1979

• A Superior Type of Flood •

W e seem to be getting more floods here lately.
Not just minor floods either; but ugly ones like you hear about
on the news, the kinds that go about capsizing house trailers, rafting
ice into bedroom windows, buckling steel bridges, and ramming big
trees across the highway.

One expects undisciplined foreign rivers like the Red and the
Mississippi to run amok now and then. But when normally mild-
mannered streams like the Saint John or Exploits or even Truro's
puny Salmon River start to act up, something's the matter.

Now when I was a youngster the floods were nice. For one thing
they always came at night, quietly. You went to bed with nothing
more on your mind than whether your latest snowman would last
overnight, and when you woke up in the morning and looked out
the window the house was on a small island in the middle of a lake
that wasn't there the day before.

And this new lake would be enormous. It would stretch across
not only Grandpa's meadow but away up to Farrell's place next door
and down to Doff Gillingham's in the other direction. In places the
water might be a good two feet deep.

It was some time before we youngsters connected this spring
flooding with the little brook in the woods back of us—in a geological
way I mean. (In this primitive outlook we resembled some of our
floodplain developers of today.) We just took it to be natural in some
years for a shallow lake to appear around New Year's or Eastertide,
just as snow usually appeared around Christmas. To us it was more
of a religious event.

Luckily (I can see now) our houses were all situated on higher ground and had no basement. This may explain the casual attitude our elders had concerning these manifestations of Nature. Except for the usual admonishments about not getting our feet wet, they left us pretty much to our own devices. We lived by the sea anyway. We knew the rules. Salt water or fresh, it seemed all the same to grown-ups.

But to us kids it made a world of difference. Our lives took on a new dimension. Listening at night to the hypnotic *slap, slap* of small waves against the picket fence outside my bedroom window, I could hardly sleep for excitement.

About the only unpleasant memory I have of those childhood events was the time I was sick in bed with the flu at floodtime. To an eight-year-old, being forced to stay indoors at all was bad enough. Being confined to bed as well, especially at such a time, seemed the height of injustice. The flood would be gone before I got better. It was a blow to my faith in the order of the universe.

However, in due course I rallied. A morning came when I could sit up in bed and hold down tomato soup and crackers. Through the scrim curtains I thought I saw some water still. The comforting lap of small waves could be heard yet. My spirits revived. Then a loud thump sounded against the clapboards outside, followed by three distinct raps below my window.

I heaved off the quilts, scrambled out of bed, and made my way on suddenly rubbery legs to the window. Squinting against the unaccustomed glare of sky and water, at first I couldn't make out a thing. A moment later my older brother's smiling features took form, almost level with my window sill. The sill was high. Had he become a giant? Was he on stilts? Mystified, I looked down and saw that he was standing in a boat.

And he was saying something that I couldn't hear. Between us we raised the window. "Want to come out in the boat with me?" he said. I was famished for the outdoors anyway. Had the house been on fire I couldn't have got dressed any quicker. As I mounted a chair the prospect of freedom steadied my knees. The shimmering vista outside banished all morbid thoughts. Holding the sash up with one hand, my brother extended the other to pilot me down.

I was halfway out the window when another hand laid hold of my britches. Our mother had other ideas. Fortunately I was considered too sick for sterner measures, but back into bed I was firmly put. As for my brave brother—who by now had retreated to a safe distance offshore—he received a severe tongue-lashing out the window for risking my life amid damp spring vapours and icy water. By the time I'd recovered, the meadow was a mess of broken ice and the magic had fled.

Still, one sour note doesn't spoil a concert. Other floods redressed the balance with other delights.

One such delight pertained to the proper testing of footgear. Adults tend to forget how important it can be to the juvenile's sense of overall security to know that new pairs of rubber boots are truly free of leaks. The only sure way to prove this is to wade them to their very rims. For this purpose the better manufacturers always finished of their boot tops with a quarter-inch red band. This line was the internationally respected Plimsoll mark beyond which we juveniles dared not trespass, on pain of forty whacks on the exposed buttocks with our wet socks. However, to stop short of that mark was to risk the scorn of one's watching peers on shore. Indeed, it was considered prudent to wet the red line itself. There could be a leak under it.

Now the superiority of a flooded meadow over the seashore for conducting these grave inspections lay in the degree of flat calm it could achieve. The seashore is never really safe. Even a minor wave or a slippery rock can swamp you. But testing on a windless day over familiar and charted back yards can proceed with due concentration and precision, and it did.

In the fullness of time one entered into the higher estate of Long Rubbers. Almost a badge of adulthood in themselves, their ownership conferred as much status on the wearer then as a driver's license does now.

One watery spring a year or two before I attained long rubber status, I persuaded my father to let me wear his for a wade on the meadow. He gave in so easily I was surprised. Perhaps he recalled his own youth. The only stipulation was that I stay clear of the ditch —whose waters would now be over my head. To this I eagerly agreed.

Of course the boots were too big for me. At first I couldn't manage them at all. But soon I found that by grasping a top strap in either hand and lifting hard at the right moment, I could Make Steps. Now I could wade beyond the range of mere knee rubbers. New worlds beckoned.

And I noticed that by unfocussing my eyes while gazing down at the quivery reflections of sky and cloud, I seemed to hover over immense deeps.... I imagined what mysterious creatures might be swimming there miles below me, creatures with slimy tentacles and rows of green and blue lights and horrible grinning jaws... and —something had me by the foot!

In taking care to avoid the ditch I'd wandered into a mud-hole. One boot was stuck fast and sinking. I started to yell for help, then thought better of it. Getting a thigh rubber wet inside was a bigger disgrace even than keeping knee rubbers dry. After all, it was only a matter of hauling the mired boot out. No need to panic. But the more I hove on that rubber, the more the other sank. And not at an equal rate. I was listing to starboard. There was only one sensible thing to do: abandon ship!

Up to my butt into the icy water I went, and pranced like a wet cat to shore. I was thankful nobody saw me. But the deed could not be hid. For one thing I was streaming wet and had to run home. Worse, out there in the water, drooping like a pair of sleepy gulls, stood the accusing long rubbers. To rescue them my father had to use the boat. That night I went to bed supperless. But secretly I exulted.

I could relate many other proofs that the floods of my childhood were of a superior type. For example, they provided unlimited scope for the making and sailing of toy boats, a thing hardly possible with today's unruly kind. Around the shores of our temporary oceans shipbuilding flourished. All available grandfathers who were handy whittlers were pressed into service, for shipwrecks were frequent. Tillers would bend and masts would splinter and paper sails would rip and ballast would shift. It was a good and happy time for youngsters and oldsters alike.

Why, even the look of the water itself was different—clear and shallow and benign as it dimpled smiling over the old snow and ice on a mild April day. Wading, you could look down then and see things with almost microscopic clarity: a cow pie lying where it fell last July with bits of golden straw catching the light, a white bone abandoned by some dog, a coat button lost in a blizzard, a prize alley long given up for lost. And, over all, the wandering crescents of liquid amber light and shadow shot through with dazzling flashes of spring sun when a breeze slid by.

No, they don't make floods like that any more.

—1976

• Grasshopper Days •

W e knew they were there. Down among the waving forest of summer grass in grandfather's meadow we could hear them. Not on rainy days or cool days we couldn't, nor early or late. But directly the sun came out and the wind shook the grass dry, then we could.

"Zztt! Zztt! Zztt!" went the grasshoppers, dry and reedy as if they needed a drink but liked the heat too much to bother. Theirs was not a song which carried far, especially if a breeze rustled the purple timothy heads and the yellow buttercups. But we children knew they were there. Listening hard, we would leave the security of the fence and wade knee-deep, waist-deep into the billowing meadow to find them.

The place to look was near the sunlit tops of the taller stems. We would spot one, then another, holding on with their spiny forelegs like British Columbia loggers on swaying spar trees or like sailors in the rigging of a windjammer, swinging with the wind as if they hadn't a care in the world. But they did, and it was us. A troop of youngsters barely able to see over the hay, we were out to catch them.

Our methods were haphazard at first. Through the tall cool grass we would come, swimming carefully with our hands, peering into the forest of stems, closing in on the solitary singers. Approaching my chosen quarry I would watch for the telltale tensing of its cocked hind legs with their pink herringbone pattern. A few steps more, a wild lunge, a wilder grab. With infinite care I would open my fist a crack and look inside. Nine times out of ten I caught only air.

Later we invented a better way, as simple as it was ingenious. One of us noticed that grasshoppers, if they got the chance, liked to sun themselves on a warm rock. We asked the obvious question— would a warm board do as well?

Poor deprived outport children though we were, lumber wasn't something we lacked. Right across the road stood Uncle Harold's sawmill. By trial and error we determined that the best kind of board was a wide flat slab with bark on its round side, one that would sit in the grass like a boat. Lay such a board in the meadow on a sunny day, go away for a hour or two, and success was guaranteed. When you came back, if you approached circumspectly and with due regard for their privacy, the board was bound to have several grasshoppers parked on it, all different sizes, all facing in different directions and all basking in the sun. And because they were drunk on infrared you could creep up and *snatch* them.

How powerful their hind legs seemed, shoving against the moist prison walls of our hands! It was nearly enough to frighten us into letting them go. But they seldom bit us. After a while we got the knack of letting them stretch out their hind legs and not letting them fold them again. We did, however, permit them to thrust their triangular faces up through the star-shaped wrinkle where our forefinger folded under our thumb. They would stare up at us and we would stare down at them, each uncomprehending of the other, the gulf between us so vast we might as well have come from different planets. Why, even their mouths didn't work like ours! Sideways jaws like a lobster's! And their biggest eyes—they had all kinds of small ones too—were made of little tiny jewels and they never blinked! What would they do for tears if they skinned a knee, we wondered. Nobody told us that the ear was located near the hip joint; but if somebody had we would have believed them.

At about this point in the staring contest the grasshopper would twitch its antenna, work its jaws a few times—and a miracle would happen. "He's makin' molasses!"

Sure enough, oozing from its mouth was a cloudy brown liquid. It did feel sticky on the fingers... was it real molasses?

"Taste it!"

We did. It wasn't. More like medicine, we decided, and best left alone. After that we felt even more respect. And now we understood the verse our grandmothers had taught us:

> Grasshopper, grasshopper,
> Grasshopper gray;

Give me some 'lasses
To put in my tay.

The other day, hoping to discover the origin of that verse, I consulted my book of Dorsetshire folklore. To my surprise it said not a word about them. Ladybugs and bumblebees, yes; hornets and dragonflies, yes, but no grasshoppers gray. Had they generated no folk sayings in the part of England where my ancestors originated? Perhaps the Dorset countryside had no such insect? Or was it too commonplace to deserve mention?

Well, no matter. We needed no folklorist or entomologist to tell us how to enjoy the grasshopper as it fiddled for us in those endless childhood days of high summer. Between our house and my grandmother's, while the ants toiled below and the world tilted toward autumn, they squandered their short lives on music and acrobatics and sunbathing. Yellow and gray and pink they were and quick as light, lauching out from dizzy top-gallant heights on their stubby wings to tumble like circus clowns into the blue-green depths, only to reappear elsewhere to climb into the sunshine again.

Oh, grasshoppers weren't our only or best summer insect. Bumblebees were good to clap into a mug with a shingle and listen to their muffled anger. Devil's darning needles were fun to knock into the brook with a branch. We caught agile black water skaters and sniffed their musky, silky white underbellies; we unearthed sowbugs or carpenters which when disturbed rolled armadillo-like into neat gray balls; we plucked white saliva globs from the grass and drew out, protesting in slow motion, the jade-green larva of the spittlebug.

About the only insects we never meddled with were the dreaded two-inch-long, black-and-white timber fly that cruised on rattling wings around the lumber piles, and the swift, copper-coloured centipede that darted away when we turned over a rock. But even they failed to captivate us the way grasshoppers did.

I think I know why. Across the gulf of evolutionary time we shared at least one thing. We felt the same about summer.

Grasshopper, grasshopper,
Grasshopper gray....

—1985

• Ice Magic •

The Inuit, we are told, have more than thirty names for what to us is ordinary *snow*. Linguists and anthropologists make much of this. But I am sure that Down East motorists have just as many names for *ice*—except that most of them are unprintable here. And little wonder. After enduring five or six months a year of what newscasters blithely term 'occasional icy patches' or 'intermittent freezing rain', after fishtailing and skidding times without number, narrowly missing this truck or that precipice (and sometimes not), what could one expect?

The other morning, scraping the knobby ice from my car windows for the tenth time this month, I was moved to reflect on how the quality of ice had deteriorated since I was a youngster. I couldn't help but note that the hard coating I was struggling to dislodge bore hardly any resemblance to the substance I remembered from childhood. The stuff under my scraper seemed a common grade, rough and unfriendly; the other was magical and somehow *amiable*. This stuff mocked my efforts and spoiled my morning; the other put a catch in my breath as I scrambled into my windbreaker at sunup on a bright Saturday morning....

Perhaps being wealthy helped—I mean wealthy in ice. Most years we had a whole Newfoundland bay full of it. This must have worried our parents. To us it was sheer delight. The two best seasons were when the ice was making and when it was breaking. Normally it started to make in December. We knew it was near when we woke and saw frost ferns on the bedroom window. As soon as I was let out I would head for the nearest ditch or puddle to check on progress. If it looked strong enough I would jump up and down on it; otherwise a rock would tell how thick it was without the risk of wet feet.

One thing that always puzzled me was how the ice formed in the first place. Often at dusk after a thaw I would squat and try to see it actually *happening*. First there was just the dark water shivering a little, and then, out of nowhere, came these little tapered transparent points, straight on one side and feathered on the other, reaching out over the quivery surface from all sides. But they never did anything while I watched. They were either there or not there. Yet by the next morning the process was complete, the crystal matrix all interlocked and cross-braced with triangular struts like a geodesic dome.

Very mysterious.

Just as mysteriously, after a few false starts, the whole Bay would catch over from shore to shore, freezing first in the coves and between islands and last down the centre where the river current ran. By January or February the ice would bear a team of horses with a load of logs. Then we didn't need permission any more.

Skates were scarce in Newfoundland around 1945. We didn't seem to miss them much. One of our favourite games was a kind of ice-boating. You simply took your sled to a lee shore on a windy day, stuck a nice bushy fir or spruce as big as you could handle between your knees, and shoved off. Man, could that sled go! Skimming across the glare ice as free as gulls, slicing through scattered snowdrifts in puffs of drifting white like summer clouds, careening on one runner as we tried to clear a frozen knob of horse manure or each other.

The only trouble was getting back home. The ideal conditions for this sport came when a frontal system dumped enough rain to coat the Bay, leaving a bitter westerly gale in its wake. However, east for us was away from home—which meant a long walk back against a stiff wind. For better footing some of us fashioned 'creepers' of nails in blocks of wood, modelled after the metal ones old ladies wore when they ventured out to Divine Service in the winter. One Sunday morning, in an ecstasy of speed like to Jonathan L. Seagull's, I ended up several miles out the Bay, alone. It was a weary trek back. Hearing the accusing chimes of morning service pealing across the ice did not help.

More mundane but just as delightful was smelting through the ice. We thought we invented it. Certainly our equipment was primitive: a piece of kindling wood with enough shop twine to reach bottom, a couple of small trout hooks, and a piece of salt beef or pork for bait. Plus the coaster, a box to put the fish in, an axe and a lunch. On reaching the right place we went ashore and cut boughs to kneel on and enough small trees to stop the wind and make it dark so we could see the smelts. When all was complete there was this very cozy feeling; no wind, a nice shelter, and down there, maybe, those lithe, silvery little fishes. Half the fun was in peering down into their dim world where olive green eel grass undulated in the tide like timothy in a summer breeze, and where every pebble and blue mussel shell was clearly visible.

If all went well we had smelts for supper.

There were some hazards. Ballicators could swallow a good-sized child or even a man if one accidentally stepped in them. Ballicators appeared where the ice had pyramided over a rock at low tide and frozen in the form of a volcano. They rose and fell with the tides, and some of them had open tops. Sometimes we slid down their steep sides.

Another hazard was rents. Rents were fissures caused by expansion. The ones along the shore were the worst, because they often let in water on a rising tide, blocking our way to shore. The offshore ones usually stayed frozen and were said to be safe. But we never really trusted them, because now and then they would boom under our feet like thunder and scare us silly.

It was years before I connected our seemingly peculiar use of the word *rent* with the word used in the King James version of the Bible to express extreme remorse: "He rent his garments." The Bay was simply rending its too-tight garment of ice.

If the coming of ice was the more magical event, its leave-taking was the more thrilling. This was due to Copying Pans, a game which entailed trotting across a stretch of water (preferably deep and wide) on an assemblage of floating ice pans (preferably small). The first to get wet was Out; the last to finish dry-shod was Winner.

During the spring breakup we copied pans before and after school and during recess. One day I decided to take the next logical step and use a pan for travelling to and from school. A quarter-mile walk by land, I reckoned the distance was shorter by sea. Choosing for my pole a nice piece of edging from the slab pile near my uncle's sawmill, I went down to the shore, picked the most boat-like pan I could find, and set out across the broad cove.

From the start the pan was surprisingly hard to push. It was also hard to keep on a straight course. When I ran to one end to turn

it, that end would start to dive like a submarine. My deck was soon awash and slippery. Worse, in my efforts to navigate I lost bottom and began to drift. Now I had a moment of panic; if a wind came up I might be blown offshore and be carried out the Bay by the steady current from The River.

By sculling and threshing about with the pole I finally managed to regain the shallow water and beach my crazy craft. The scare kept me on dry land for a whole week.

Copying Pans marked the end of the major ice events in our year. Next thing we knew only a few pans were left stranded along the shore like beached whales and dripping their life away in the suddenly warm sun. Even the few snowbanks were getting too sugary to make a decent snowball. This might have troubled us, except that already the small brooks in the woods sang of trouting and swimming, already the barn-soiled sheep, heavy with lamb, were out searching for the first blades of green. It was Spring.

Spring took our minds off the Ice.

Although the quality of ice has declined a great deal since I was a youngster, this at least has not changed; Spring still takes my mind off it.'

Hurry up, Spring.

—1977

• Cod Oil and Cocomalt •

By rights we should have been laced with a birch switch and sent to bed with no supper.

But we were still too young to manifest a social conscience, and besides, our parents didn't always know what we were up to. So we thought nothing of taking perfectly good cod liver oil, sent by the government to improve our health, and pouring it in the Bay. Worse, we felt we were only doing our duty. It was only cod oil, wasn't it?

The idea that we were willfully destroying government property and wasting taxpayers' money never occurred to me then.

The government nurses who came to our isolated Newfoundland village once or twice a year on the hospital boat *Bonnie Nell* to pull teeth and snip tonsils had determined that we were, of all things, undernourished. No doubt we were, some of us more that others. There was seldom a cow in the place, and when there was, we had no way of telling if it had TB. Goats and hens weren't that common either. Our main sources of protein were salt beef and wild meat and fish.

So some kind soul in the British Commission of Government, which ran Newfoundland's affairs after the financial collapse of 1935, came up with this scheme of injecting more vitamins and minerals into our diets by daily doses of hot chocolate and cod liver oil. The schools were to administer the program. Thus it came about that, sometime in the 1940s, on one of the last trips of the coastal steamer before winter closed in, some mysterious crates arrived at our school. Inside them were big canisters of cocoa and stout bottles of cod liver oil. I think the cocoa was withheld until after Christmas. But the cod oil was issued forthwith.

We had seen the stuff before, in Fogo. There each fisherman kept a barrel near the splitting table, and chucked the cod livers into it as they worked. The smelly oil would rise to the top, where it would be skimmed off and used. Likely this government oil was made the same way! Only now it was all done up in a handsome square-shouldered blue flask with a black screw top. If you held a full bottle to the light and squinted through it, the world took on an ugly shade of green. But an empty bottle turned everything the colour of choppy seas on a fine day. I think the label said 'Munn & Company, St. John's, Nfld'.

"Now boys and girls," said our gray-haired spinster teacher, holding a bottle aloft for all to see, "here's your cod liver oil. Be sure to take it right home after school today, and put it on a high shelf where the little ones can't reach." (We couldn't imagine why they would try.) "And don't forget," she continued, "to take one teaspoon full after every meal without fail, and to always wipe the mouth of the bottle after, so the oil won't get strong." (We couldn't imagine it any stronger.) Then, smiling deliberately, she demonstrated by sipping a spoonful herself. We were impressed.

But she was wasting her breath and her taste buds. We had no intention of letting the stuff pass our lips if we could help it. At least not for the vitamins. Of course we were well aware of its stirling qualities. From the cradle up our parents had drilled them into us, along with such dietary maxims as 'Fish is Brain Food' and 'Liver Strengthens the Blood'. Still, we couldn't just acquiesce. We cast about for ways to assert our independence.

One way, oddly enough, was to take an overdose. This form of one-upmanship (one-downmanship?) was reserved for boys. The game was to see how much you could chugalug and still keep your natural colour—and your last meal. The most I ever downed at one go was a third of a bottle.

Much more satisfactory was greasing our boots with it. Most of us lived handy the seashore, so our leather footgear took a beating from the salt water. We spent many hours in wet socks. Here cod oil was a godsend. True, its waterproofing qualities didn't compare with those of *Dubbin*. And it stank. But it was free, so we poured it on generously and laughed when the cats went delirious over us.

By far the best way to use up cod oil was to feed it to the Carey Chicks. Carey Chick was our name for the petrel, a small blackish seabird named for its habit of seeming to walk on water like Saint Peter. (None of us knew or cared then where the local name originated, but years later I learned that it came from 'Mother Carey's Chickens', which in turn derived from *Mater cara*, Latin for 'gentle mother'—because Old World sailors believed these birds to be under the special care of the Virgin.) However, Newfoundland seamen regarded petrels as bad omens, from their habit of hanging around ships in distress.

We youngsters welcomed the sight of them. They usually arrived with the first easterly gale in the fall, when the wind spat cold rain and churned the Bay to a froth and smashed waves against the rocks and drove the tattered clouds inland over the sodden bogs and forests. Out of nowhere they would appear, bounding among the waves like swallows, planing a few inches above the rough water without wetting a feather, looking as if this was their favourite weather. You couldn't call them a pretty bird. But they flew like the wind.

Which is why we found them so hard to hit with a rock. We slung rocks at them till our arms were hove out of joint or until the recess bell dragged us away. Not only were the Carey Chicks too fast for us (they even seemed to enjoy all the splashing and shouting), but they mostly stayed out of range.

Here again our vitamin supplement came to the rescue. We discovered that Carey Chicks, being fish eaters by trade, also relish cod oil. We found that if we poured a little on the water they would sometimes veer our way and flutter over the slick, trying to scoop some up in their bills. And if we got them doing this in close enough, we might just bring one down.

I don't recall that we ever did. A few years ago someone brought me a small seabird to identify. It was sooty brown with a white rump, and had this funny tube on its beak. I was stumped until I looked it up in Tufts' *Birds of Nova Scotia* and found it was a petrel. Had we killed one I'm sure I would have recalled that strange beak. It's one hunting failure I take some comfort in.

Once the weather cleared, the birds would vanish as swiftly as they had come. By then most of our cod oil ration was gone too.

But we still had our cocoa. "Now children, " the teacher would chirp as she twirled the lid off a fat canister of premixed cocoa and milk and sugar before recess time every winter afternoon, "let's all sing our *Cocomalt Song*. Remember it's sung to the tune of *Jingle Bells*. One, two, three...."

And as she spooned the beige powder into a great copper kettle that hissed and spluttered on the wood stove, we would launch into the chorus:

Cocomalt, Cocomalt,
That's what we all say;
Every boy and girl should drink
A glass or more each day!

There were several verses in the same vein. We sang them all, while the teacher stirred with her wooden spoon and steam gently fogged her glasses and her dignity.

What nameless bard penned those verses I may never know; but the chorus has stuck in my mind long after more sublime stanzas from Milton and Shakespeare have slipped away. It shows the power of a good tune.

By the time we had sung the last verse the brew was ready. Filling a white enamel jug from the kettle, Teacher would go stooping from mug to mug around the room until all three dozen of us had been ministered to. Then, like English matrons sipping afternoon tea, we would sit at our desks and take our Iron and Calcium. It was hard to imagine us as bloodthirsty petrel hunters then. Cocomalt brought out the best in us—as cod oil brought out the worst. But no wonder; it tasted about ten times as good, and the song made us happy. No one could blame us.

Or could they? What about all those quarts of liquid sunshine sacrificed to boots and birds? After all, the government was only trying to help. And as government programs go, it wasn't bad. It was well conceived and well executed, and it reached down to the point of need without being sapped along the way. In the few years it operated it went far to cure the ills that plagued outport children in those pre-road, pre-Medicare days; tooth decay, anemia, rickets, scurvy, TB.

At least the *Cocomalt* half of the program did. The cod oil half, thanks to our sabotage, accomplished little more than keeping our feet dry and our aim sharp.

May the worthy Commissioners, not to mention Munn and Company, forgive us.

—1978

• The Portage Road •

Thirty—no, forty—years ago, in the long sweet days of child-hood, when the sky was never so blue and the snow never so white and every day was a week long, I had a friend. A lanky quiet boy who loved the woods and brooks, he was descended from a long line of woodsmen and rivermen and their seacoast wives. Second cousins we were, of the same age, and in some strange way closer than brothers.

Our homes were a scant hundred yards apart as the crow flies, yet it seemed farther than that when we were ten, and with the alder swamp between us we had to go the long way around to visit. Visit is not really the word, for more often we met indoors solely to plot some ramble outdoors, staying only long enough to make the customary responses that adults expected, then darting away with knapsack and lunch and whatever other accoutrements the season demanded, an axe and rabbit snares in winter or a fishing rod and bait in summer.

It is the fall and winter forest rambles I remember best and treasure most. We lived in a community surrounded by wilderness. To the west, the nearest village was fifteen miles through lake and forest country, to the south nearly two hundred miles. The men of our community logged, guided, hunted and trapped. So the woods were second nature to us, as natural a playground as fields to a farm child. Our parents allowed for this. Though a city parent would have been alarmed at our freedoms, in reality we were less at risk than children who dodged cars and trucks.

Every Saturday morning that was civil, my friend and I would rush through our chores, filling woodbox and water barrel and feeding hens and dogs in haste, eager to be on the trail. If it was in the fall, our goal would be to check for rabbit signs in certain places and to set our first snares of the season. Meeting at some convenient point, we would take the Portage Road and head southwest.

Now The Portage Road was just that—a road over which, thirty years previously, supplies of food and hay and tools were toted each fall to lumber camps in the interior. But at ten or twelve our minds were almost innocent of any history that went back farther than our own. To use its name was merely a code for this particular narrow winding path that led farther and farther from home, and of whose final destination we knew naught because we ourselves had not yet seen it with our own eyes. It might as well have been called The Porridge Road. Explorers and discoverers ourselves, we were busy giving it a new history that suited our imaginations. Like kittens exploring the room in which they were born, week by week we pushed back the frontier. Whereas, at ten, we dared not let the village out of our sight, now we ventured a mile, two miles and more into the woods. Once or twice we even came home after dark. Nothing attacked us. Our confidence grew. In time we knew every inch of that winding narrow trail that led to Rushy Pond and beyond. And in imagination I can still see it.

Leaving the community road, you crossed a plank bridge over a small stream and hurried (if you were small) by the low, dilapidated dwelling of a crotchety, red-eyed old man who sometimes bawled oaths at us (though of course *we* had done nothing to deserve it). Then you crossed a small and rocky meadow kept close-cropped by roving sheep and goats, and passed through some young fir and spruce woods, until the road dipped to a narrow bog where dwarf black spruce grew and clumps of Labrador tea and carpets of spongy sphagnum moss were turning wine-red before winter.

By and by you came to Big Hill, from where you could catch a last glimpse of the village. And just off the trail to the south was a lone pine in an opening, one of the very few white pines left in those parts, and if you detoured you could feel its rough platy bark and admire its unclimbable trunk soaring to a tufted, sparse evergreen crown that soughed in the breeze like the waves of the sea. Intersecting the path a bit farther on was a small brook. Just upstream someone had hollowed out a place to dip drinking water. If you happened to be thirsty, you might halt here under the spruce trees